Simon Fraser, after whom the Fraser
River is named. In 1808 Fraser and his
Voyageurs explored the river from what is
today Prince George to the ocean. During his epic
canoe journey he named the Thompson River after his
friend, explorer David Thompson, although Thompson
never did see the river which bears his name.

# FRASER &
# THOMPSON
# RIVER
# CANYONS

## FRONT COVER

The photos are of the Trans-Canada Highway ascending Jackass Mountain, see page 75, and the bridges at Alexandra.

The suspension bridge, built in 1926, is on the site of the original built by the Royal Engineers in 1863. The Engineers bridge was the first suspension bridge in Western Canada and a famous landmark on the Cariboo Wagon Road. (See page 62.)

## PHOTO CREDITS

B.C. Provincial Archives, 36, 47, 48, 52-53, 64-65, 68, 74, 79, 82, 111, 119, 124; Expo 86, 6, 7; Glenbow Alberta Institute, 44-45; Tom W. Hall, 31, 84; Hell's Gate Air Tram, upper inside front cover; National Film Board of Canada, 114; New Westminster Museum, 12; Public Archives of Canada, 56 (C7656), 78 (C29881), 108 (C180); Tourism British Columbia, front cover, lower inside front cover, 14, 115, 118; Vancouver Public Library, 60, 87, 104-105; Richard Wright, 31. All other photos: Heritage House.

## CANADIAN CATALOGUING IN PUBLICATION DATA

Main entry under title:

Vancouver-Kamloops through historic Fraser and Thompson River Canyons.

ISBN 0-919214-76-2

1. Trans-Canada Highway — Guide-books. 2. Fraser Canyon (B.C.) — Description and travel — Guide-books. 3. Thompson River Valley (B.C.) — Description and travel — Guide-books.
FC3845.F73V3 1986    971.1'33    C86-091099-7
F1089.F7V3 1986

HERITAGE HOUSE
PUBLISHING COMPANY LTD.
Box 1228, Station A
Surrey, B.C. V3S 2B3

Printed in Canada

## INDEX

## FOREWORD

Most of the historical background in this book was researched by author-broadcaster C. P. Lyons and appeared in his popular *Milestones on the Mighty Fraser*. Originally published in 1950, the book was reprinted several times but went out of print in the late 1950s. Since then massive changes have taken place in B.C., including a completely new highway through the Fraser Canyon, a four-lane highway from Vancouver to Hope, with another four-lane, $375 million highway from Hope to Kamloops scheduled for completion in 1987.

Side roads, in particular, are in a constant state of flux because of changing logging and mining activity, with old roads abandoned and new ones constructed. On roads used by logging trucks travellers should exercise extreme caution, obey all signs and carry a current, detailed map.

On main highways there are also changes. Communities are bypassed; Stop-of-Interest signs moved and new ones added; Tourist Information Centres, both government and community, change locations; new Provincial Parks are built and similar variations occur. For these reasons, this guide is intended to be a general reference only.

Few regions in North America have such a wealth of varied scenic beauty and romantic historical interest as British Columbia. In the many thousands of square miles that go to make up this most westerly province, no more interesting combination of history and scenery is found than along the Fraser and Thompson River Canyons. Happy travelling.

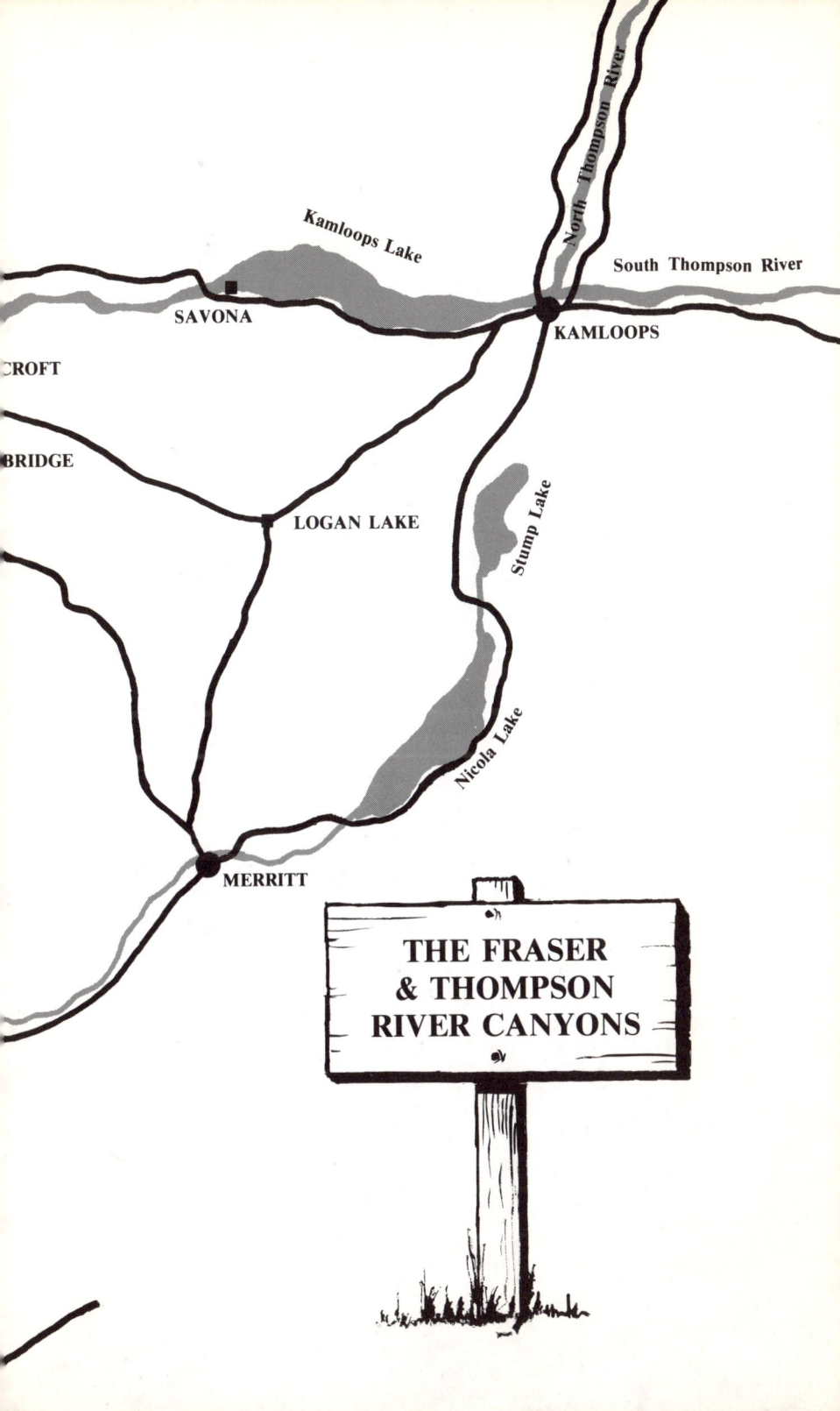

# route data

## VANCOUVER TO KAMLOOPS

Vancouver 0 miles (0 km) — Kamloops 268 miles (431.5 km)
**Vancouver, population 410,000,** is unique in its rapid development from small frontier outpost to Canada's third largest city. Within the memory of many of her citizens, the tangled web of forest became a vast pattern of streets and buildings. Here is a brief historical sketch:

1862 — Hugh McRoberts pre-empted 160 acres (65 hectares) of land

now partly occupied by the Marine Drive Golf Club. In the same year a young Englishman, John Morton, chose a hole in the dense forest and built a cabin near the site of the Marine Building in the downtown area on the waterfront.

1863 — A discerning Royal Engineer turned down a land grant in favor of an oil painting for a wedding present. How was he to know that the land would become the city's business center and be worth not millions of dollars but hundreds of millions?

1884 — The early settlement was called "Gastown" in honor of a loquacious character known as "Gassy Jack."

1886 — The city of Vancouver was incorporated on April 6. Two

**Vancouver, Canada's third largest city.**

months later, on June 13, fire almost completely destroyed the pioneer community.

1887 — On May 23, the first trans-continental Canadian Pacific Railway passenger train arrived from Montreal.

1888 — Stanley Park was reserved as a park.

1891 — By this year, a water system had been installed, electric lights introduced, and a street-railway charter granted. CPR Empress liners connected Vancouver with the Orient.

1913 — Between 1905 and 1913 a real estate boom led to a period of great expansion. In 1891 the population was under 14,000; by 1911 it was 100,000; by 1921 over 160,000. This expansion slowed during the Great Depression of the 1930s, although by then the population had doubled from the 1920s to nearly 350,000. Since World War Two the city has grown steadily and dramatically. Today it is the commercial hub of B.C. and its nearly three million people, about one-half of whom live within commuting distance in surrounding communities such as West and North Vancouver, Burnaby, New Westminster, Richmond, Surrey, Delta, Langley, Abbotsford and Chilliwack.

## LOCAL PLACES AND NOTES OF INTEREST:
### Visitor Information:
Two sources of information, one for the city, one for the province, are less than three blocks apart in the downtown area. For complete information on Vancouver call at the Greater Vancouver Convention and Visitors Bureau in Royal Centre at 1625-1055 West Georgia Street. Phone: 682-2222.

Tourism British Columbia, the official government tourist center, is in the Robson Square complex at 800 Robson Street, two blocks from the Vancouver Visitors Bureau. It provides maps and similar literature on all of B.C. and is open year round. Visitors should be sure to pick up a copy of *Accommodation Guide* which contains a description and rates for most provincial motels, hotels, holiday resorts, fishing camps, trailer courts and much more. Phone: 660-2300.

Other Tourism British Columbia offices are at the Vancouver International Airport and the B.C.-Washington crossing point of Douglas at 356 King George Highway, Surrey.

**With towering snow-capped mountains,** the ocean at the end of many streets, the green Fraser Valley behind, and the mild Japanese current protecting it from the harsh winter common to the rest of Canada, Vancouver offers a bewildering variety of activities. Hiking, golfing and salmon fishing are year-round activities; skiing in winter is only minutes away; there are revolving restaurants, massive shopping centers, major sporting events and a host of other attractions.

**There is, for instance,** the winter and summer playground of Grouse Mountain which rises behind the city. It is only fifteen minutes from the city center over the massive arch of Lions Gate Bridge to the enclosed skyride which takes visitors to the 3,700-ft. (1,100-m) level with its winter skiing, summer alpine flowers and year-round panorama of Vancouver, the Fraser Delta and the Strait of Georgia.

As the above photo taken in the early 1900s indicates, Vancouver businessmen have long appreciated the value of visitors and worked to make them feel welcome.
Mountain scenery, below, is one of the city's attractions.

**Stanley Park** offers 1,000 acres (400 ha) with miles of trails, a zoo, aquarium and Lost Lagoon with its wild waterfowl which include comparatively rare trumpeter swans. The aquarium is open all year and introduces visitors to over 6,000 salt- and fresh-water species. The star attractions are the killer and beluga whales in the marine mammal complex. They perform throughout the day, the killer whales showing remarkable intelligence and agility for such large creatures.

**The Vancouver Museum and Planetarium** complex is only ten minutes from the downtown area. Here in photographs and exhibits visitors re-live the city's history from the days of the early explorers in 1741 through 1865-1890 when it was essentially a mill town to the turn of the century when Vancouver began its impressive growth.

**The Maritime Museum** part of the complex is home to the *St. Roch,* the historic RCMP schooner which was built in Vancouver in 1928, and in 1940-42 became the first vessel to sail from west to east through the ice-choked Northwest Passage of Canada's Arctic. In 1944 she set another record when she became the first vessel to sail through the Passage from east to west. The *St. Roch* has been fully restored and is today a National Historic Site.

**Included in a host** of other attractions are the 60,000-capacity, $126 million B.C. Place covered stadium; the Capilano Salmon Hatchery; the George C. Reifel Waterfowl Refuge with its thousands of waterfowl; and much more, including Canada Place, a waterfront complex visited by over 150 passenger liners a year.

In addition to free brochures, maps and guides available at the Tourist Bureau, there are at least five major bookstores within two blocks of Robson Square. Books about Vancouver range from full color guides to those describing walks in the city and hikes in the surrounding mountains, and from how to catch salmon to the city's colorful history.

**Our mileage** starts in downtown Vancouver and leaves via Georgia Street, past B.C. Place Stadium to Main Street, Commercial Drive, then 1st Avenue.

Vancouver 5 miles (8 km) — Kamloops 263 miles (423.5 km)
**Junction — 1st Avenue and Trans-Canada Highway:** For westbound travellers the Trans-Canada crosses Burrard Inlet then continues through North and West Vancouver to Horseshoe Bay. Here travellers board one of the B.C. Government's Ferries which can carry upwards of 400 vehicles and 1,500 passengers for a two-hour voyage across Georgia Strait to Nanaimo on Vancouver Island. Then the Trans-Canada Highway heads southeastward some 75 miles (120 km) to Victoria, B.C.'s capital and western Mile Zero on the nearly 5,000-mile- (8,050-km-) long highway.
Eastward to Hope the Highway is four-lane.

Vancouver 8.5 (13.6 km) — Kamloops 259.5 (417.9 km)
**Exit to Deer Lake Park and New Westminster:** In Deer Lake Park just off the freeway is Burnaby Village Museum, a re-creation of a typical village

along the interurban railway of 1890-1925. Over thirty buildings from a General Store to Finlayson's Pharmacy, from the Royal Bank to a village church preserve artifacts and re-create the atmosphere of pioneer days in the Lower Mainland. Open from March to the last Sunday before Christmas. Phone: 294-1233.

Vancouver 12.9 (20.6 km) — Kamloops 255.1 (410.9 km)

**Exit to New Westminster and Highway 99A:** New Westminster, population 40,000, was the capital of the Crown Colony of British Columbia in the 1860s when Vancouver Island was also a Crown Colony and Vancouver twenty years in the future. Its history dates to 1850 when a couple of hardy pioneers settled on the sloping banks of the Fraser River. The community originally was called Queensborough, but later the name New Westminster was selected by Queen Victoria. The first buildings appeared in 1859.

As a combination seaport and supply point for the vast interior of B.C., the new community prospered. For nearly thirty years it was the most important on the mainland coast but was bypassed when the CPR was completed to Burrard Inlet in 1886. A new community called Vancouver was born and New Westminster waned. Then on September 10, 1898, occurred a calamity that befell virtually ever pioneer settlement — fire. A headline in the local paper noted:

"ROYAL CITY TERRIBLY DEVASTATED BY THE BIGGEST CONFLAGRATION IN THE HISTORY OF THE PROVINCE: Saturday, September 10, 1898 will ever be memorable, a red-letter day in the history of the Royal City, writ in lurid letters of leaping-flame, which, on that ill-fated night, between an hour before and two after midnight, laid a third of the city, including the entire business portion, in blazing ruins, and rendering hundreds of people, for the time being, homeless, and many practically destitute . . . ."

The city was rebuilt but destined to be eclipsed by the upstart Vancouver — except for sports. Because of its winning teams, the community calls itself the City of Champions, best known for its lacrosse victories. The New Westminster Salmonbellies have won more national box lacrosse championships than any other team. Appropriately, the city is the home of the Canada Lacrosse Hall of Fame.

In the past decade, New Westminster has been involved in a redevelopment project that is one of the largest in Canada. First phase was construction of a new Law Court, then came completion of Douglas College. The third phase, still in progress, is redevelopment of the main waterfront with emphasis on people. When completed it will provide over 1,000 housing units, hotel, waterfront market and riverfront esplanade along more than a mile (1.6 km) of river front.

LOCAL PLACES AND NOTES OF INTEREST:

**Visitor Information:** The Tourist Information Centre is at 333 Brunette Avenue just off the freeway exit. From June to September it is open every day, and from September to May on Monday to Friday. Phone 521-7781.

**Irving House Historic Centre:** Completed in 1864, this house is a direct link with the sternwheeler steamers and lumbering freight wagons of the Cariboo

Visitor attractions in the Lower Mainland range from the Fraser Valley Trout Hatchery near Abbotsford, largest in B.C., to Irving House Historic Centre at New Westminster. Constructed in 1864 by pioneer Fraser River steamboat captain William Irving, the house is almost unchanged, its fourteen rooms furnished to represent the era from the early 1860s to the 1890s. Behind the house is New Westminster's Museum which has two floors of exhibits.

gold rush. It was built by Captain John Irving, the most famous of the sternwheel captains and a respected citizen known as "King of the River." Although Captain Irving died in 1872, his descendants lived in the house until 1950. Then it was purchased by the city to become New Westminster's first official heritage building. It is a charming window to history, its fourteen rooms furnished to represent the period 1864-1890. At 302 Royal Avenue, it is open in summer from Tuesday through Sunday, on weekends the rest of the year. Phone: 521-7656.

**New Westminster Museum:** Conveniently located behind Irving House, the museum contains two floors of exhibits. Of extreme historical importance is the Dufferin Coach, built in 1876 to carry Canada's Governor-General Lord Dufferin some 400 miles (640 km) up the Cariboo Wagon Road from Yale to the Cariboo goldfields. Thereafter it served as a B.C. Express Company special coach for travellers too impatient to wait for the regular stagecoach.

*Samson V* **Maritime Museum:** Sternwheel steamers were a feature of the New Westminster waterfront for nearly half a century. In fact some old-timers believed that the fire which destroyed New Westminster in 1898 was started by a spark from a passing sternwheeler. While the cause is unknown, it did start at the waterfront and destroyed three sternwheelers.

The *Samson V* was the last sternwheeler to ply the Fraser. Built in 1937, she was a Federal government boat used to clear debris from the Fraser River. When her service ended in 1980 she was turned over to the City. Today photos and other artifacts portray the sternwheel era, while her original galley and cabins illustrate what life was like on a working sternwheeler. She is moored on the waterfront between 8th and 10th Streets and is open weekends. Phone 521-7656.

**From New Westminster** Highway 99A heads across the Fraser River over 1½-mile- (2.4-km-) long Pattullo Bridge. Eight miles (12.8 km) to the south is the border and the Customs points of Douglas and Blaine. Peace Arch Park with its lawns, flowerbeds, and fine picnic facilities is located at the International Boundary, Blaine.

NOW RESUMES ROUTE DESCRIPTION OF THE TRANS-CANADA HIGHWAY:
Vancouver 15.3 miles (24.5 km) — Kamloops 252.7 miles (407 km)
**Exit to Highway 7:** This highway is an alternate route to the Fraser Canyon via the west bank of the Fraser River. It is paved and passes through the communities of Port Coquitlam, Haney, Mission and Agassiz, rejoining the Trans-Canada Highway some 100 miles (160 km) to the northward just west of Hope.

Vancouver 16.7 (26.8 km) — Kamloops 251.3 (404.7 km)
**Port Mann Bridge and the Fraser River:** The Fraser is the longest river lying entirely within British Columbia. It is 790 miles (1,270 km) long, or about 2½ times the distance between Vancouver and Kamloops. Its drainage area, over 91,000 sq. miles (235,690 sq.km), gathers almost twenty-five per cent of B.C.'s rain and snow run-off and funnels it through the mountains in a mighty brown flood. Here it is over one-half mile (1 km) wide.

The graceful Port Mann Bridge is over one mile (1.6 km) long with a 54-ft.- (16-m-) wide roadway and two sidewalks with lights concealed in the handrails. It was one of nearly 800 bridges, tunnels and such projects built during the over $1 billion Trans-Canada Highway reconstruction program in the 1960s.

Vancouver 21.2 (34 km) — Kamloops 246.8 (397.5 km)
**Exit to 176 Street and Highway 15** through Cloverdale to the U.S. border and Interstate Highway 5.

Vancouver 22.5 (36.1 km) — Kamloops 245.5 (395.4 km)
**Memorial Tree:** Eastbound travellers will notice a slight curve in the freeway and a tall fir stump covered with ivy. The fir, a memorial to those in the district who served in the Flying Corps in World War One, was in the path of the freeway but engineers deviated to avoid the then still growing tree.

Vancouver 24.3 (38.9 km) — Kamloops 243.7 (392.6 km)
**Exit to Langley and Fort Langley National Historic Park:** Langley, population 15,000, is the center of a rich farming and dairying district. The name is from the old "Fort Langley" which, in turn, was named after a Director of the Hudson's Bay Company. The first explorers described this region as "a little plain" and found it excellent for growing vegetables, hay and grain. It was known to them as the "Big Prairie."

**Fort Langley National Historic Park,** about 3 miles (4.8 km) north of the freeway on the east bank of the Fraser River, is a major historical site. The following background information is courtesy of Parks Canada:

"The original post was built by the Hudson's Bay Company in 1827 because George Simpson, the Company Governor, felt the establishment of a new depot near the mouth of the Fraser River would end American competition, control coastal trade and protect the Company's interests in the interior. The post succeeded, and by underselling American competition, dominated trade with Indian tribes throughout Vancouver Island, the Fraser River and Nootka Sound.

"Simpson also assumed that the Fraser River would be the gateway to interior posts, but the Fraser Canyon proved to be too much of an obstacle.

"Fort Langley retained its influence in Company operations by diversifying its activities. Salmon-packing became a flourishing industry and farming on Langley Prairie expanded until Langley Farm was a major producer of provisions for Company posts and ships.

"A new post, built upstream in 1839, closer to Langley Prairie, was destroyed by fire and rebuilt in 1840. This became the site on which Fort Langley National Historic Park was reconstructed.

"The only surviving structure from the fort's past, the storehouse, served as the cooper's shop, and is now set up as the H.B.C. store. Other fort buildings have been reconstructed to help make the park an authentic reflection of the fur trade era on the West Coast."

Since Fort Langley was intended to be a supply area, in 1828 the first horses and cows on what is today mainland B.C. were put ashore to start an agriculture industry. In 1925 during ceremonies dedicating an historical cairn, C. H. French of the H.B.C. described this era:

For westbound travellers, Bradner Road Rest Area west of Abbotsford has facilities which include washrooms and a B.C. Government Information Centre open all year. On the opposite page is a replica of the "Big House" at Fort Langley National Historic Park where in 1858 B.C. was born, although it was then the Colony of British Columbia.

"What wonderful men were these old fur-traders! The more one knows about them, the more one wonders how it was possible to gather such picked men together at these remote spots. It took years to get supplies, and for many years one mail each year was as much as could be expected. Ordinary wages would not do it. They had to subsist on the natural resources of the country, and on that account one can readily understand why such feverish haste was made to establish farms where potatoes, cereals, beef, butter, etc., could be raised to supply not only Langley, but other posts farther inland.

"Langley, then, became a food depot of no mean size where a large number of servants were employed; a depot for storing furs while they were being gathered for transportation to London. It was considered the only safe place on the coast from Russian molestation during the Crimean War, 1854-56.

"Langley was the original exporter of salt salmon. She exported hemp to England to be made into rope. Langley was the first to make and export barrels. She sent large consignments of cranberries to San Francisco during the fifties. Langley made milk-pans from birch-bark, brooms from birch-sticks pounded into strips at one end; also horse-collars, wedges, axe-handles, mall-handles, toboggans, etc., from birch. Langley ground flour from wheat with crude stones. Her blacksmiths made locks, hinges, axes, and many other articles required in the trade and for the use of the posts."

Since the Fort was a supply center, through its palisades passed the voyageurs — the world's finest canoemen; personnel from wilderness posts such as Fort St. James which could be weeks of travel away; and Indians in cedar-bark clothing. In 1858, however, there appeared a different class. They were the gold seekers, mostly from California, drawn to the Fraser by the discovery that its gravel bars were incredibly rich. They heralded the end of the fur trade era.

An English author, Kinahan Cornwallis, described one of them:

"He was a gaunt, stringy, dried up looking Kentuckian, with a gutta-percha coloured face, sunk into which, on either side of his nose, twinkled two all alive and piercing eyes. His hair was long and light, and crisped up with the dry heat of the weather, so much so that it gave me the idea of extreme fragility and brittleness. He carried a couple of revolvers, and a bowie knife, with the point of which he took the opportunity of picking his teeth immediately after supper."

Another writer in June 1858 described the incoming Americans in the following words: "They were all 'packed', that is, they all carried more or less baggage across their shoulders, and were all equipped with the universal revolver, many of them carrying a brace of such, as well as a bowie knife."

The flood of miners surging up the Fraser River caused considerable apprehension to James Douglas, Governor of Vancouver Island. They were virtually all Americans, and Douglas knew that unless British law was enforced, incidents might arise which could result in United States annexation of the area. Douglas knew, too, that his jurisdiction over the mainland was tenuous at best, and even if he had full powers over the area, he had no way of enforcing that power.

Fortunately, the summer passed without serious challenge to his authority and by autumn his problems had been solved by the British government. He was appointed Governor of the new Colony of British Columbia and sworn in by Judge Matthew Begbie at Fort Langley on November 19, 1858.

With the Fraser River gold rush and the subsequent stampede to the Cariboo in the early 1860s, new communities appeared and Fort Langley was bypassed. It closed in 1886 and the site deteriorated. In 1923 it was declared of national historic interest but nothing was done to preserve it and the old buildings continued to decay and disappear. In May 1955, however, the site was declared a national historic park and restoration begun.

Today, the Fort with its reconstructed palisades and blockhouse; the "Big House" where Governor Douglas became Governor on that rainy November day in 1858 and other buildings; men and women dressed in period costumes; and the axes, blankets, beads, barrels and other artifacts of the fur trade attract tens of thousands of visitors annually. The Fort is open all year with the exception of December 25-26 and New Year's Day.

**The Hudson's Bay Company:** This famous Company owes its origin to two dissatisfied French trappers who, upon being forbidden by French fur traders to exploit the Hudson Bay country, interested a group of Englishmen in the fur trade. In 1670, Prince Rupert and seventeen associates secured a charter for "The Governor and Company of Adventurers of England trading into Hudson Bay". Authorized to expel rivals, build forts, and to declare war and peace, the infant Company was financed on a capital of $52,500, divided into thirty-five shares.

Usually in the forefront of exploration and commerce, the Hudson's Bay Company expanded westwards across Canada. Then, in 1824, the confusion brought about by rival fur-trading concerns on the Pacific Coast, and the threat to the new land from the United States, resulted in action from London. HBC Governor Simpson was ordered across the continent to survey the situation.

As a result, in December 1824 Chief Factor James McMillan and thirty-eight men set out to find the Fraser River, explore its possibilities for a fort, and chart its outlet. Travelling northward from Fort George at the mouth of the Columbia River, they found the entrance to the Nikomekl River before reaching the Fraser. Indians advised them it was possible to proceed up this winding river and, by making a portage, reach the Fraser.

Probably this 4.5-mile- (7.2-km-) portage passed through Langley Prairie and over much the same route as the present road leading to Fort Langley. The last few miles (kilometers) to the Fraser were made by following the crooked little waterway now known as the Salmon River.

After exploring upstream for some 20 miles (32 km), the voyageurs paddled to the mouth of the Fraser and made soundings which showed sufficient depth for navigation. So it was that this expedition of 1824 laid the foundation for the establishment of Fort Langley, the first fort on the Lower Mainland north of the 49th parallel.

Vancouver 28.8 miles (46.2 km) — Kamloops 239.2 miles (385.3 km)

**Exit to Highway 10 for Vancouver International Airport** and B.C. Ferries Tsawwassen terminal for Swartz Bay and Victoria, B.C.'s capital.

Vancouver 33.6 (53.9 km) — Kamloops 234.4 (377.6 km)

**Exit to Aldergrove and Highway 13** south to the border and Customs points of Sumas-Huntingdon. Aldergrove, population 2,500, is the business center for the sprawling farming district that stretches to the border.

About one-half mile (1 km) south on Highway 13 is **Vancouver Game Farm**. The Farm, open from 8 a.m. to dusk every day, is home to nearly 100 species from around the world, including tigers and elephants. Lots of parking, washroom facilities, picnic area, lunch counter and gift shop.

**Geology of the Fraser River Delta:** From Vancouver and almost to Hope, 100 miles (160 km) away, the Highway crosses a huge, fan-shaped flat. Known generally as the Fraser River Delta, this 1,000-sq.-mile (2,590-sq.-km) flat is built from the tremendous volume of eroded material brought down by the river during millions of years. It is estimated that the sediments are approximately 3,000 ft. (900 m) in depth.

The Highway crosses several broad, flat-topped plateaus before reaching Abbotsford. These rise about 400 ft. (120 m) above the general elevation and represent the height of the delta after the last glacial period. They now stand as remnants left by the river which in its ever-changing course has cut away the surrounding ground. Most of the delta is covered with highly fertile soil forming over 5,000,000 acres (2,035,000 ha) of agricultural land.

One fascinating aspect of Fraser River geology is that about 15,000 years ago it was in the grip of the last ice age. Most of Canada and the northern United States were covered in a sheet that was probably 10,000 ft. (3,000 m) thick in the northern region but "only" 5,000 ft. (1,500 m) deep in the Fraser Valley. This ice mass depressed the land hundreds of feet (meters). The Strait of Georgia wasn't salt water as it is today, but a massive fresh-water lake extending from the Fraser Valley to Vancouver Island, and from Quadra Island to Puget Sound, some 200 miles (322 km). But as the ice melted the land rose, the Strait as we know it was formed and Vancouver Island became surrounded by salt water.

When the ice disappeared from the Fraser Valley about 10,000 years ago, nomadic groups from the south appeared and gradually worked up the Valley. Some 9,000 years ago they started fishing for salmon which became their staple food.

Vancouver 36.8 (59.3 km) — Kamloops 231.2 (372.2 km)

**Note to Westbound Travellers:** On your side of the divided freeway is **Bradner Road Rest Area.** This is a major development with washrooms and flush toilets, sani-station, phones and a large parking area with picnic tables. There is also a B.C. Government Tourist Information Centre which is open all year. A panel gives the following background about the area's original inhabitants:

FOOD AND COOKING OF THE NORTHWEST COAST INDIANS
"The rich Northwest Coast environment provided a variety of foods for the Indian inhabitants. Fish, along with land and sea mammals, were the

18

principal foods. This diet was supplemented with shellfish collected from the beaches and food such as berries, fern roots and camas bulbs.

"There were several methods of cooking these foods. Boiled meals were heated in water-tight wooden boxes or baskets by means of heated stones which were lifted from the fire with wooden tongs and dropped into the container. A second method was steam cooking, using large shallow pits lined with hot stones. Food was placed on the rocks, covered with leaves and mats, and soaked with water to produce steam. Fish and meat were also roasted over the open fire, baked on beds of coals, or dried for future consumption.

"The main meal of the day was prepared in the late afternoon, although food was available for snacks at any time.

"Each meal usually included two main dishes — a boiled liquid food served in a wooden bowl and eaten with spoons, followed by meat or fish, served on small cedar bark mats and eaten with the fingers."

Vancouver 39.5 (63.5 km) — Kamloops 228.5 (368 km)

**Exit to Abbotsford Airport:** Here in mid-August is held the Abbotsford International Air Show, one of the largest in the world. For over twenty years tens of thousands of spectators have watched world renowned aerobatic displays and all of the other attractions of a major air show.

**Golden Ears Peaks** (Mt. Blanshard) stand prominently about 20 miles (32 km) to the north. They form the jagged 5,600-ft.- (1,680-m-) high terminus of one spur of the Coast Range, and lie within the southern portion of Golden Ears Provincial Park.

These twin peaks were often featured in Indian legend. In summer months when the air was usually clear they were visible from the ocean and so marked the period of the salmon-run. This was the signal for the Indian tribes to make their way up the delta to the favored fishing grounds.

Although the mountain is officially called Mt. Blanshard after Richard Blanshard, the first Governor of Vancouver Island, it is more popularly called Golden Ears. This name apparently was first used in the late 1850s by Captain George Richards, a British naval officer who was certain that gold was abundant in the region. If gold is there, it remains undiscovered, although the snow-peaked area now yields gold of a different value.

As Golden Ears Provincial Park the mountainous region is part of a massive recreational facility centered on beautiful Alouette Lake. It has 344 vehicle campsites, wilderness walk-in campsites, a variety of hiking trails, picnic areas, sani-station, boat launching, change house, large sandy beach, and a park naturalist in summer. Golden Ears is accessible by a 10-mile (16-km) paved road from Highway 7 on the west side of the Fraser River.

**Mt. Baker,** 10,750 ft. (3,359 m) and perpetually snow-capped, is 28 miles (44.8 km) to the south. It is the northerly peak in a series of magnificent volcanic cones that extend down the Pacific Coast into California. These mighty peaks of which Mt. Lassen, Crater Lake, Mt. Shasta, Mt. Hood, and Mt. Rainier are examples, form a chain of relatively recent volcanoes. Their glaciers, snowfields, flower-meadows, and forests have made them favored recreational and scenic areas of the Pacific Northwest.

Mt. Baker, despite its ethereal crown of snow and ice, must have a

**The Trans-Canada Highway and the Fraser Valley in the Sumas area. At Chilliwack, opposite page, mountains close in, the Highway skirting the landmark of Mt. Cheam.**

hot heart. Two vents, or fumaroles, near its summit continually force out steam and sulphurous vapors.

**Early Travel Routes:** While speeding along this fine Highway a person may wonder how the early travellers made their way. In those days the navigable section of the Fraser River proved the easiest and cheapest route of travel. Highlighted by the urgency of moving men and supplies to the goldfields in 1858, service by river steamers was inaugurated. Although the famed Cariboo Wagon Road was completed to Barkerville in 1865, it was many years before there was a Lower Mainland road connection to Hope.

As late as 1873, the only land route between Fort Langley and Chilliwack was the Hudson's Bay Company foot trail, described as a soggy track over damp ground and unbridged streams. Not until a year or so later was a road completed from New Westminster to Hope.

Vancouver 42.1 (67.7 km) — Kamloops 225.9 (363.8 km)
**Exit to Clearbrook**, a modern community surrounded by rich farm land.

Vancouver 44.1 (71 km) — Kamloops 223.9 (360.5 km)
**Exit to Abbotsford:** The communities of Clearbrook and Abbotsford which center a population of some 60,000 are called "The Hub of the Fraser Valley." The land is rich and the climate moderate; in fact, local boosters claim that the area enjoys the best average temperature in Canada. Strawberries, blueberries and raspberries are important crops with the region growing 90 per cent of Canada's raspberries. The Abbotsford Berry Festival, held in late June, celebrates the annual harvest. Nearby Bradner is renowned

for its extensive daffodil fields, with tens of thousands of blooms shipped to still frigid Eastern Canada every spring. Bradner's April Daffodil Show has attracted visitors for over forty-five years. For further information contact the Abbotsford-Clearbrook Chamber of Commerce, 2462 McCallum Road, Abbotsford, B.C., V2S 3P9.

Vancouver 45.4 (73.1 km) — Kamloops 222.6 (358.4 km)
**Junction of Highways 1-11:** Southward on Highway 11 is the U.S. border at Huntingdon-Sumas, and northward across the Fraser River is Mission on Highway 7, an alternate paved route to either Vancouver or the Trans-Canada Highway near Hope.

**Fraser Valley Trout Hatchery** is about 2.5 miles (4 km) southward down Highway 11 then west on Vye Road. The province's largest trout hatchery, it annually hosts some 35,000 visitors and features a self-explanatory viewing area with displays of live trout, illuminated photos, glassed-in walkway overlooking the fry-rearing area and a theatre with hourly slide shows and films. Phone (604) 853-8394 for hours of service.

From Vancouver the Trans-Canada has been angling southeastward but now gradually heads northeastward to eventually pass through Kamloops, Banff and Calgary towards its destination of St. John's, Newfoundland. Not until it reaches Ontario some 2,000 miles (3,220 km) away will it again be this far south.

Vancouver 49.6 (79.8 km) — Kamloops 218.4 (351.7 km)
**Cole Road Rest Area** with washrooms, sani-station, phone, picnic tables

21

and lots of parking on the eastbound — Hope — lane of the freeway. (For westbound — Vancouver — travellers, Bradner Road Rest area is on your side of the freeway 13 miles (21 km) ahead. It has washrooms, lots of parking, phone, sani-station and a B.C. Government Information Centre.)

Vancouver 53.2 (85.7 km) — Kamloops 214.8 (345.8 km)
**Exit to Cultus and Chilliwack Lakes:** Cultus Lake, 10 miles (16 km) southward over a paved road, is one of the most popular lakes in the Lower Mainland. The main reason is Cultus Lake Provincial Park with four campgrounds containing 300 units. There are picnicking areas, boat launching ramp, sani-station, and opportunities for outdoor activities which include swimming, fishing and hiking.

Chilliwack Lake is about 30 miles (48 km) away close to the border. Part of the road is paved, the rest gravel. Chilliwack is a beautiful 5-mile- (8-km-) long lake set amidst mountains which rise over 7,000 ft. (2,000 m). At Chilliwack Lake Provincial Park is a 100-vehicle campsite with picnicking area, sani-station and boat launching ramp. Recreational activities include hiking, swimming and fishing for rainbow, cutthroat and Dolly Varden.

Vancouver 55.2 (88.9 km) — Kamloops 212.8 (342.6 km)
**Sumas Drainage Canal:** Dairy herds graze and crops grow richly on the fertile land of Sumas Prairie stretching from the Highway for several miles (kilometers). At one time, however, ducks settled by the thousands on a shallow lake that spread over this entire area. Sumas Lake was imprisoned between Sumas Mountain, the base of which the Highway skirts, and Vedder Mountain, 3 miles (4.8 km) away on the opposite side of the valley.

The reclamation of these 30,000 acres (12,140 ha) was accomplished in 1924 by dyking the entrance point against the flood waters of the Fraser River and channelling the flow of two incoming streams. The lake waters were then pumped out and a main drainage channel dug for the area. As the bottom of the reclaimed lake is nearly 3 ft. (1 m) below mean sea level, it is easy to see how susceptible to flooding is this flat country.

**The Great Flood of 1948:** "The 80-Mile-Long Valley of Misery" was the descriptive name given to this section of the Fraser Valley after a late spring, heavy rains, and rapidly melting snows caused the river to overflow its banks. Thousands of fertile acres (hectares) disappeared under the eddying flood waters, and roads, telegraph lines, power lines, and railroads were submerged. The Fraser Valley was completely cut off from communication with the Interior.

Gradually the muddy water receded, leaving in its wake a landscape of soggy desolation. Once green pasture lay crushed and colorless under a brown scum that clung grimly to everything touched by the waters. Gardens, berry plants and even orchards were brown specters of once pastoral scenes. The exact flood height was painted on every structure in mud. Fortunately, the rich soil was quick to show its recuperative powers, and by the fall of 1948 a green carpet once more clothed the fields.

Vancouver 56 (90.2 km) — Kamloops 212 (341.3 km)
**The Vedder Canal:** This Canal is bounded by a giant dyke to prevent the

Vedder River from inundating the rich reclaimed land. The Vedder River is the lower section of the Chilliwack River, named after Volkerk Vedder who crossed the continent by ox-team and arrived in the Valley in 1856.

**Mountain ranges** are fast closing in on either side. The system to the southeast is known as the Cascade Mountains; that to the north, the Coast Range. This latter chain, averaging 100 miles (160 km) wide and stretching northwards along the B.C. coast for 900 miles (1,450 km), is fully as rugged as the Rockies.

Mountain systems can be formed in several different ways. Each method involves gargantuan forces that make an H-bomb seem like a firecracker. The surrounding mountains are formed from rocks that once were molten and which were forced or "intruded" into the upper parts of the earth's crust. Before reaching the surface they cooled and, since the cooling process was relatively slow, the rock particles had time to group into large crystals. This distinctive "granular" construction has given the name "granitic" to this type of rock. Such a large intrusive mass is known as a batholith. Thus we get the technical geological term for the Coast Range — "an intrusive granitic batholith."

Over millions of years, erosion has worn the envelope of old rocks from the granite and carved the familiar peaks and valleys we now see.

The mountains, while beautiful, are subject to sudden weather changes which has earned the region the title "The Graveyard of the Air." The worst disaster occurred on December 9, 1956, when a four-engined Trans-Canada Airline's plane disappeared. Despite a massive search that lasted for weeks, no trace of the aircraft or the sixty-two people on board was found. The fate of the plane remained a mystery for five months until three mountaineers, climbing 8,200 ft. (2,460 m) Mt. Slesse (the prominent jagged spire to the south of the Highway), found wreckage from the missing aircraft. Because of the extreme hazard of both rock slides and avalanches, none of the bodies was brought out. They are still on the mountainside, Mt. Slesse their imposing memorial.

Vancouver 60.3 (97.1 km) — Kamloops 207.7 (334.4 km)
**Exit to Lickman Road and Chilliwack Chamber of Commerce Hospitality Centre:** Both northbound and southbound travellers can exit from the freeway via Lickman Road to this friendly and informative Hospitality Centre. Open daily from 9 a.m. to 8 p.m. during the summer, 9 a.m. to 5 p.m. the rest of the year. As part of visitor information the Centre has a TV video with clips showing Manning Park, Harrison Lake and other attractions in the area which local boosters call "Rainbow Country." Facilities include 12 picnic tables, washrooms, parking for RVs, pet area, and a mini-forest which features all trees native to B.C. In addition, nearby buildings house a display of antique farm machinery. Phone (604) 858-8121.

Vancouver 62.4 (100.5 km) — Kamloops 205.6 (331 km)
**Exit to the communities of Sardis and Chilliwack, Cultus and Chilliwack Lakes, and Canadian Forces Base.** The city of Chilliwack and the township of Chilliwhack (spelled with an extra "h") are home to some 50,000 people, the Upper Fraser Valley's major centers. Interest in this area was broken

For eastbound travellers Cole Road Rest Area near Abbotsford has lots of parking, picnic tables, phone and washrooms.

Chilliwack's Hospitality House Tourist Centre is open all year and accessible from both east and west traffic lanes.

by several long intervals after Simon Fraser in 1808 passed on his eventful journey down the mighty river. Even with the establishment of Fort Langley almost twenty years later, it was another twenty-five years or so before Volkert Vedder, in 1856, drove his cumbersome ox-team onto this beautiful Indian domain of "Chil-uk-wey-uk," or "Valley of Many Streams."

The gold rush of 1858 saw thousands of miners heading up-river. Among them were some who saw promise in the succulent grasses that fringed the river banks. These men of foresight made a promise to return should the mining prove disappointing. In 1862 Jonathan Reece, a butcher at Yale, perhaps prompted by thoughts of obtaining his meat locally rather than from far away Oregon, persuaded several friends to stake land with him at Chilliwack. Their pre-emptions coincided with the area now occupied by the city.

Settlement proceeded rapidly. The first group of houses, built near the river, was known as "The Landing." Then in 1873 the settlers on the scattered farms and ranches decided to unite, making Chilliwack the first incorporated rural municipality in British Columbia. Before long, business moved farther inland from the river and a new settlement called "The Corners" appeared. It grew so rapidly that by 1877 it was renamed Centreville. Expansion continued and the name was again changed, this time to Chilliwack which was incorporated as a village in 1883. Imbued with optimism, however, citizens set aside some 2,000 acres (810 ha) for a city, despite much ridicule from larger centers. In 1908 the village became the city of Chilliwack.

Development since that date is well evidenced in the prosperous business district and fine homes. The surrounding fertile land produces fruits, field crops and vegetables in never-ending abundance, while the lush pastures are home to sleek dairy herds.

**Canadian Military Engineers Museum:** From the exit continue south on Vedder Road 3 miles (5 km) to the Canadian Forces Base. Items dating back to 1610 which preserve the history of the Military Engineers are on display, including weapons and uniforms from the Zulu and Boer Wars. Of particular interest is the life-size replica of a Royal Engineers sitting room containing authentic pieces of period furniture. (See Mile 112.7 for information on the Royal Engineers who arrived in B.C. in 1858.) Hours of opening vary. Phone (604) 858-3311.

Vancouver 64.4 (103.7 km) — Kamloops 203.6 (327.8 km)
**Exit to Prest Road and Rosedale:** The mountains are closing in on both sides, with the Highway now skirting rugged 6,925 ft. (2,080 m) Mt. Cheam. The most impressive view of the peak, however, is from Highway 7 which follows the west bank of the Fraser River. Geologists believe that near here the Fraser once emptied into the ocean. The river's delta is still expanding some 10 ft. (3 m) a year and in 6,000 years (more or less) will have built a land bridge across the Strait of Georgia to Vancouver Island.

Vancouver 72.2 (116.3 km) — Kamloops 195.8 (315.2 km)
**Junction of Highways 1-9 and Bridal Falls Tourist Area:** Highway 9 heads west across the Fraser River via Agassiz to Harrison Lake.

Four miles (6.4 km) from the Trans-Canada it crosses Highway 7, an alternate route to Vancouver or the Trans-Canada Highway just west of Hope. Along Highway 7 it is 23.5 miles (37.6 km) to the Trans-Canada via the west side of the Fraser.

**Kilby Historic Park:** This park is on Highway 7 some 8 miles (12.8 km) west of the small community of Agassiz. At Kilby visitors from rural centers can re-live their past in the country store that is the Park's central theme.

The "T. Kilby Hotel and General Store" opened in 1904 and was operated by the Kilby family for nearly seventy years. Then, because of its historic significance, it was purchased by the Provincial government. Visitors can see long forgotten brands of food on the time-worn shelves and goods of all kinds hanging from the ceilings — even play checkers by the pot-bellied stove. In summer the store is open daily.

As part of the Historic Park there is a parks campsite on the bank of the Harrison River with 38 units, change houses and boat launching ramp.

**Harrison Lake:** From its junction with Highway 7, Highway 9 continues about 6 miles (10 km) to Harrison Lake and Sasquatch Provincial Park. Harrison is the Lower Mainland's largest lake, some 35 miles (56 km) long and in 1858 was part of the original route to Cariboo. The route was short lived, being abandoned when the Cariboo Wagon Road was completed through the Fraser Canyon in 1863. Today Harrison is extremely popular with recreationists who have a choice of luxury accommodation at a world-renowned spa or camping in the wilderness.

**Harrison Hot Springs Hotel:** This resort in its mountain setting is noted for its fine golf course, excellent swimming and fishing, and its mineral spring swimming pools.

**Sasquatch Provincial Park:** Though the park is named for the legendary Sasquatch, or Bigfoot, visitors are most likely to see more familiar creatures such as beaver and deer. The park is on the east side of Harrison Lake some 5 miles (8 km) from Harrison Hot Springs. It includes three campgrounds: Bench with 75 units; Lakeside with 25 units on Deer Lake; and Hicks with 30 units on Hicks Lake. There is also an extensive day-use area on Harrison Lake with picnic tables, boat launching ramp, swimming, and fishing in Harrison Lake. Fishermen should remember, however, that like all big mountain lakes, Harrison can get rough very quickly.

**Sasquatch — Is they is, or is they isn't?** Indian lore has it that a mysterious race of giants known as the Sasquatch live in the high mountains around Harrison Lake. Over the years, Indians have reported brief encounters with these individuals. Such stories are not easily discounted, for the Indians have a remarkable memory for detail, and find little purpose in distorting the facts as they know them.

The following story is only one of many told by Indians, although white people have also reported seeing the creatures:

"Over a hundred years ago, when the Indians were berry-picking, a woman who had strayed from the others was suddenly confronted by a giant. Too paralyzed with fear to scream or run, she was quickly carried up the steep mountain side. After a long climb, during which time she remained in a semi-coma and did not note direction or length of time, she was carried through a rough door into a large rock cave.

"Two other Indian women were crouched in the cave and, when left alone with the new arrival, told her they had been captured in a similar manner years ago. They had been brought as wives for the giants and had since borne children.

"The men would disappear for months at a time and then return with food. For the new woman they brought flour and smoked fish that they knew she was accustomed to eating. (The fact that there was flour dates the story as taking place after the arrival of the Hudson's Bay traders, 1827-1840.)

"Although the woman was a captive for over a year and bore a child, she was determined to escape. The other two women told her they would help and when the hairy giants left on one of their seasonal hunting trips she was told to prepare all the food she could. She made bread, or bannock (suggesting that these people of the Indian women at least used fire) and with a heavy pack of food set out across the mountains.

"After almost unendurable hardships she became exhausted and was carried and helped along by the other two women who possessed the giants' strength in some measure. She was left in a stupor near where she had originally disappeared.

"The villagers saw her but she suddenly became afraid of them and fled. She was pursued and carried to her father's house where she fainted and remained under a spell. The Indians believed that the giants held some mental power over her but with careful nursing she eventually recovered."

The Sasquatch legend is one that refuses to die. Over the years dozens of newspaper accounts have appeared, several books have been written and even film footage shot in the U.S. of what was supposed to have been Bigfoot. Despite all the publicity, the mystery remains — "Is it is or is it isn't?"

**The junction of the Trans-Canada and Highway 9** is also the access road to Bridal Veil Falls Tourist Area with attractions which include Bridal Veil Falls Provincial Park, Bedrock City and Minter Gardens.

**Bridal Veil Falls Park** has picnic tables in a forest setting and a majestic waterfall which cascades into the valley. A viewpoint at the falls is only a 15-minute stroll through a magnificent cedar and fir forest.

**Flintstones Bedrock City** is a tourist attraction based on the characters of a popular comic strip that will appeal to children — perhaps of all ages.

**Minter Gardens:** From April until October these Gardens are filled with dazzling color from acres of flowers ranging from those in the Alpine Garden to the Rose Garden, from the Meadow Garden to the Fragrance Garden. Services include ample parking, washrooms, gift and garden shop, and food.

SOME WILDLIFE:

**Chipmunks and squirrels** are probably the most widely known of the small mammals. Between Coast and Interior, the motorist will likely see two kinds of squirrels. Through the Fraser Valley and part way into the Canyon, the Douglas squirrel is in its habitat, easily recognized by its orange-colored

From its junction with the Trans-Canada, Highway 9 heads over the Rosedale-Agassiz Bridge to the west bank of the Fraser River. It provides access to Minter Gardens, Harrison Hot Springs and Highway 7, an alternate route to Vancouver or Hope.

belly. The red squirrel, however, is a native of the Interior. Its under-parts are a whitish grey, making quick identification possible.

Chipmunks are smaller than the squirrels and spend most of their time on the ground. Very active and quick, they are the "cutest" of animals to watch. The species living on the Lower Mainland is the Townsend chipmunk, a rather dark-colored animal, almost as big as a squirrel. The Columbian chipmunk of the Interior is smaller and much more colorful with conspicuous tan and grey stripes.

**The Coast, or Columbian, black-tailed deer** ranges over the Lower Mainland and probably northwards into terrain with definite Interior vegetation. It seldom weighs over 180 lbs. (80 kg), about one-half that of the mule deer which inhabits the entire Interior Plateau and is characterized by exceptionally long mule-like ears.

**Coyotes and opossum** — the latter not a native species — are fairly common in the Fraser Valley, while in the surrounding mountains are black and grizzly bears, mountain goat and moose.

SOME FLOWERS AND TREES:

**The ox-eye daisy** is a large white daisy that raises its showy bloom among the tops of the high grasses. Like many roadside flowers, it is not a native.

**Field chamomile** is a frequent companion of the ox-eye daisy. While the flowers are similar, it is not as tall and has many small branching stems. Blooming dates for both are from June 1 to August 15.

**Goldenrod,** a high plant with a conspicuous tuft composed of small yellow flowers, makes an appearance along the Highway toward the end of August. It continues from the Fraser Valley well into the Canyon. Some species once were used as a source of yellow dye.

**Dogwood trees** are very prominent during May with their rich cream-colored flowers. This beautiful tree grows so profusely over the Lower Mainland and Vancouver Island that it was chosen as the provincial floral emblem.

**Mock orange, or syringa,** ornament their graceful branches with clusters of fragrant creamy-white flowers. Blooming during June and the first half of July, it graces Highway borders well into the Canyon. Indians valued the young straight shoots for arrows and, in some parts of the West, used the ground-up leaves to produce a thin lather of soap.

**Red elderberry** is an early bloomer, so its massed heads of small white flowers won't be seen after the end of April. However, its bunches of bright red berries are so flauntingly displayed during July that it can't be overlooked. Those with a fondness of elderberry wine should not pick the red berries since they may exhibit poisonous qualities. The black berried elder is the one to use.

**The Coast maple** is a shaggy giant of a tree with a thick gnarled trunk and ponderous limbs. In keeping with its size are the leaves which often measure 12 inches (30 cm) in length and width. As a general rule, however, the really large leaves are found on the young shoots. The tree favors rich moist soils and is found up the Fraser Canyon to beyond Boston Bar. It is a valuable hardwood tree widely used in the furniture industry.

**Black cottonwood** dominates the other roadside deciduous trees by reason of its large high trunk and lofty irregular branching crown. The bark on old trees is rough and deeply fissured, but on young trees it is smooth and green.

NOW RESUMES ROUTE DESCRIPTION OF THE TRANS-CANADA HIGHWAY:
Vancouver 87.9 (141.6 km) — Kamloops 180.1 (289.9 km)
**Hunter Creek Rest Area** on the eastbound (Hope) lane of the freeway has picnic tables and rural toilets on a section of the original Fraser Canyon Highway. There is also access from the westbound lane.

**Side Roads and Back Roads:** From the Trans-Canada between Vancouver and Kamloops radiate hundreds of miles (kilometers) of roads, ranging from paved to excellent gravel to cow country byways. While ordinary vehicles can be used on many without a problem, some require better clearance than that provided by the average family car and, at times, four-wheel drive is reassuring. A potential problem with many of the less travelled side roads is the lack of signs. For this reason it is important for drivers to have detailed maps. In addition, road guides will make the trip much more pleasant — and a lot less confusing.

An excellent series is *Lower Mainland Backroads* by Richard and Rochelle Wright. There are four volumes in the set, each providing mile-by-mile (and kilometer-by-kilometer) data, with information on camping places, flora and fauna, history, fishing and similar material.

Volume 1 covers from Garibaldi to Lillooet via Squamish and includes the Bridge River and Yalakom country.

Volume 2 describes ten back roads from New Westminster to Hope in a variety of one- and two-day trips.

Volume 3 provides data on back roads from Hope to Clinton, an area not only particularly rich in them but also one where it is comparatively easy to get lost.

Volume 4 is of the Garibaldi region and describes eleven routes easily accessible from Vancouver.

An excellent general map covering from the Okanagan west to the Garibaldi area, and from Vancouver to the southern Cariboo is *Vancouver-Kamloops,* published by the B.C. Ministry of Environment. This map and others are available at most government offices and commercial map outlets. For a complete index of available maps write: Survey and Resource Mapping Branch, Ministry of Environment, Parliament Buildings, Victoria, B.C., V8V 1X5. Phone 387-1441.

The Federal government publishes an excellent series of topographical maps of Canada. For an index write: Geological Survey of Canada Publications, 100 West Pender Street, Vancouver, B.C., V6B 1R8. Phone 666-0271.

The Outdoor Recreation Council of B.C. produces a regional series of maps which show campsites, hiking trails, river and lake access, and similar information. They are available at commercial outlets or by writing: The Outdoor Recreation Council of B.C., 1200 Hornby Street, Vancouver, B.C., V6Z 2E2.

For people calling at either the Greater Vancouver Convention and

While the chipmunk, left, is found throughout B.C., the raccoon is more selective and largely confined to Vancouver Island, the Lower Mainland and the Okanagan Valley.

Visitors Bureau or Tourism British Columbia in downtown Vancouver, two commercial map outlets are nearby. One is World Wide Books and Maps, 949 Granville Street, phone 687-3320. The other is Dominion Map Ltd., 541 Howe Street, phone 684-4341.

Vancouver 93.3 (150.3 km) — Kamloops 174.7 (281.2 km)
**Exit to Skagit Valley Recreation Area.** Twenty-four miles (38.6 km) away over a gravel road, this wilderness area has 44 campsites plus walk-in camp-sites and a wide variety of outdoor activities that include canoeing, fishing, hiking and nature study. The mountain-ringed Valley is not only home to many kinds of wildlife, but also the most westerly stand of Ponderosa pine in Canada and rare wild rhododendrons.

Vancouver 95 (153 km) — Kamloops 173 (278.5 km)
**Junction of Highways 1-3.** Highway 3 is an historic route that threads across southern B.C. to the Alberta border. (See Heritage House book, *The Dewdney Trail.)*

Vancouver 95.5 (153.7 km) — Kamloops 172.5 (277.8 km)
**Hope,** a bustling community of some 4,000 in the snow-capped Coast Mountains. It has a wide variety of tourist services and justifiably calls itself "Gateway to the Interior." The Trans-Canada heads up the Fraser Canyon to Kamloops and eastern Canada; Southern Trans-Provincial Highway 3 roller-coasters eastward across several mountain ranges to the Rockies and Alberta; and the Coquihalla Highway heads northeastward to Merritt and Kamloops.

Hope has a rich historical background, first settled by fur traders in 1848 when the Hudson's Bay Company built a fort, one of several in the isolated interior of what became the province of British Columbia. These forts used centuries-old Indian trails and myriad waterways for communication. Horse brigades of the Hudson's Bay Company, taking their yearly supply of furs eastward, followed the Columbia River from headquarters at Fort Vancouver in what is today Washington to Boat Encampment at the top of the river's Big Bend in B.C. where it turns southward in its journey to the Pacific. From there they crossed the Rockies by way of Athabasca Pass while the "outfit" of supplies and trade goods for the following year returned by the same route. When the Oregon Treaty of 1846 placed the lower Columbia River in the United States, however, officials of the Hudson's Bay Company had to look for trails in British territory. Accordingly, the trading post of Fort Hope was established in 1849 at the junction of the Coquihalla and Fraser Rivers. It was intended to be the converging point for the horse brigades from posts in New Caledonia 400 miles (640 km) to the north and from Fort Colvile and Fort Okanagan on the Columbia to the southeast.

The Hudson's Bay Company built a stockaded fort which dominated the waterfront and at times close to 500 people congregated at Fort Hope. During such occasions it was a bustling place with members of brigades loading furs on boats to go downriver to Fort Langley, or assembling out-fits to be placed on packhorses for shipment to the Interior. Prominent pioneer trail builder Edgar Dewdney described it thus: "When all the packs were made up and things were in shape for the return journey, the fun commenced and Indians and voyageurs put on their best clothes, the half-breeds and some of the officials in their leather dresses and beads with streamers of all colors from the hats. Dancing and horse racing were the principal amusements.''

After the gold rush to the Fraser River in 1858 when some 30,000 hopeful miners stampeded to the region, a townsite was laid out near Fort Hope by the Royal Engineers. They also built a small frame church of lumber milled locally and hand-planed. Glass, carpets and fixtures came from England around Cape Horn. Fathers of the Oblate Mission supervised the building of another church near the Indian reserve, although in 1860 Father Grandidier wrote of the new town: "Poor Fort Hope! It is poorly named. It is dull, slack, deader than a door nail in spite of three steamboats which come twice a week to rouse it from its lethargy.''

But that same year Hope appeared ". . . a charming, busy little place, nestling in the mountains'' to the eyes of fifteen-year-old Susan Moir, newly arrived from England with her mother and stepfather and her elder sister, Jane. She noted ". . . a pretty little church and parsonage, a Court House, HBC fort and store, hotel, saloon, two stores, a butcher's shop and blacksmith shop.''

## LOCAL PLACES AND NOTES OF INTEREST:

**Visitor Information:** For visitors an excellent first stop is the combined Hope Museum and Tourist Information Office on the Trans-Canada Highway in Hope. The museum has many artifacts depicting Hope's fur trade and mining background, including a gold ore concentrator and antique mining equipment. Direct links to the fur-trade era are a wooden Hudson's Bay Company sign and an old Company flag typical of those which fluttered from forts across Western Canada to the Arctic.

**Christ Church** at the corner of Fraser Avenue and Park Street only a few blocks from the museum ranks among the oldest in B.C. The lumber for it was sawn at a nearby mill established in 1859, one of the earliest sawmills in B.C.

The church is a tribute to the Reverend A. D. Pringle who arrived at Hope in 1860 and began a subscription drive to raise funds. From miners, judges, merchants and even the Governor of B.C., James Douglas, he raised some $2,700 — more than enough since his new church and furnishings cost $2,353.40. It was consecrated in November 1861. The first marriage was in 1864 when Edgar Dewdney (who built the Dewdney Trail which is today's Hope-Princeton Highway) married Jane Moir.

The church has been in use since it opened, although it was restored and re-dedicated in 1958.

**The "H" Tree:** Four blocks along Hudson Bay Street from the Trans-Canada is the "H" tree, formed some eighty years ago when someone entwined the limbs of two trees. In true legendary fashion, the "someone" was supposed to have been twin girls who planted the tree, then tied a ribbon round the trunks.

**Kawkawa Lake Provincial Park:** About 2 miles (3 km) east of Hope over paved Kawkawa Lake Road, this popular day-use park offers swimming,

Fronting the Trans-Canada Highway in Hope, the Museum and Tourist Information Centre are easily accessible. A few blocks away amid fir and cedar trees is Christ Church, consecrated in 1861. One of B.C.'s oldest churches, it is still in use.

On Kawkawa Lake, lower right, is Kawkawa Lake Provincial Picnic Site with picnic tables, piped water, boat launching ramp and change rooms.

fishing and picnicking. There is a large public beach with free launching ramp, change rooms, toilets, piped water and picnic tables. Every year the lake is stocked with several thousand rainbow trout and kokanee (small landlocked sockeye salmon). Anglers should remember that they need a valid freshwater fishing license and to check the current B.C. Sport Fishing Regulations.

**Othello Tunnels:** These tunnels on the abandoned Kettle Valley Railway can be reached by turning off Kawkawa Lake Road onto Othello Road. They are a visible link to the days when the echo of the steam engine's whistle reverberated through the mountains flanking the Coquihalla Valley.

**Memorial Park:** Located in the center of Hope just off the Highway, this park features picnic tables and a playground with plenty of room for car-weary children, pets and parents.

**Historical Cairn:** On the river bank in Hope is the cairn FORT HOPE: "To commemorate the building of a stockaded post at Hope by the Hudson's Bay Company in 1848 and the opening of a way into the interior through British Territory. By the 'Brigade Trail' eastwards from Hope trade was maintained for twenty years; until, with the finding of gold on the Fraser River, the valley awoke to greater activity and new highways were brought into use."

NOW RESUMES ROUTE DESCRIPTION OF THE TRANS-CANADA HIGHWAY:
Vancouver 96.3 (155.1 km) — Kamloops 171.7 (276.4 km)
**Fraser River and Bridge:** This double-deck bridge is the only one of its kind in B.C., with the CPR on the lower level. Although the railway's mainline is on the west side of the Fraser, this spur was part of the now abandoned Kettle Valley Railway which served southern B.C. via Princeton, Penticton and Nelson.

Vancouver 97 (156.1 km) — Kamloops 171 (275.4 km)
**Junction of Highways 1-7:** For travellers bound to Vancouver, Highway 7 bypasses Hope along the west bank of the Fraser River and rejoins the Trans-Canada over the Rosedale-Agassiz Bridge (See Mile 72.2), or can be followed right to Vancouver.

Vancouver 98.6 (158.7 km) — Kamloops 169.4 (272.8 km)
**Lake of the Woods Rest Area:** Picnic tables and toilets on the lake shore. This small lake is stocked regularly with rainbow trout and is a peaceful place because power boats are banned.

**Tansy:** No, it isn't a species of fish in the lake. It is the showy bright yellow flower which flanks the Highway and blooms during the latter part of August.

Vancouver 100.2 (161.3 km) — Kamloops 167.8 (270.2 km)
**American Creek and Bridge:** Here the Canadian Pacific Railway parallels the Highway so closely that motorists can almost chat with the train crew. The CPR and the CNR tracks, like the Highway, cling to the Fraser and Thompson River valleys all the way to Kamloops.

**The Canadian Pacific Railway:** Why was a transcontinental railway built from Eastern Canada during 1880-85 across several thousand miles of country which was largely unexplored and sparsely settled? B.C. at the time had a population of only 10,000 white people, and what is today Alberta and Saskatchewan had virtually no whites. A clamor from B.C. was the reason.

By 1865 the gold rush had waned and the population was eager for new development. In 1866, the two colonies of British Columbia and Vancouver Island united and began clamoring for a road link to Eastern Canada. Then, the U.S. purchase of Alaska left many people wondering if this faraway corner of the British Empire might not be next in line, heightening the urgency for action.

In 1867, the Legislative Council asked Governor Seymour, "... to take measures without delay to secure the admission of British Columbia into the Canadian Confederacy." An essential condition to such admission should be "... the construction by the Dominion Government within two years, of a transcontinental wagon road, connecting Lake Superior and the head of navigation on the lower Fraser River."

Instead of a wagon road, several plans for constructing a railway to the Pacific were advanced by groups of financiers, but after much bickering and considerable political repercussions it was decided that the Canadian government would build the railway. From then on, the project was known as the Canadian Pacific Railway. After incurring tremendous expenses, the Canadian government was forced to let a private company take over the financing.

From Hope to Alexandra Bridge, Highway 1 and the Canadian Pacific Railway are never far apart as they wind along the west bank of the Fraser River.

At left is railway contractor A. Onderdonk and the sternwheel steamer *William Irving* at Emory Bar between Hope and Yale in the early 1880s. Then the site of the flamboyant construction town of Emory City, it is today a popular provincial campsite.

The rail tracks reached Port Moody on July 4, 1886, and the first train from Montreal arrived in Vancouver on May 23, 1887. Today, the CPR, still managed by a private company, has grown into one of the world's major transportation systems.

Vancouver 105.9 (170.5 km) — Kamloops 162.1 (261 km)

**Emory Creek and Bridge:** All is peaceful here now but in the 1880s when construction of the CPR started the wild west community of Emory City sprang up. It had thirteen streets, two hotels, and nine saloons — evidently not enough to quench the railway workers' thirst because there was also a brewery. The first newspaper published on the B.C. Mainland was cranked out in 1880 and the first locomotive in B.C. was unloaded from a sternwheel steamer at the creek mouth for use in CPR construction.

**Andrew Onderdonk, the Master Railway Contractor:** Apart from Rogers Pass, the toughest section of CPR construction in B.C. was the 127 miles (204.4 km) between Emory Creek and Savona's Ferry. It was built by Andrew Onderdonk, a young United States engineer, and for many years it was known as "Onderdonk's Railway."

Since most of the line was to be built with picks, shovels and wheelbarrows, Onderdonk needed upwards of 10,000 men. The nearest source of this labor was California, but many of those who came for the $2-a-day pay quickly proved unsuitable. They soon earned the name "Onderdonk's Lambs," — but not because they were passive.

The first batch of some 200 whites arrived in March 1880. A few days later the newspaper at New Westminster, the *Dominion Pacific Herald,* reported: "Of Onderdonk's 'Frisco boys who went up to Yale last week, 12 were in the lock-up the first night and 20 the second."

Confronted with an obvious labor problem, Onderdonk imported 2,000 Chinese from China in two boatloads of 1,000 each. They were paid $1 a day and proved so conscientious that eventually most of the 7,000 men who were on Onderdonk's payroll at one time were Chinese.

For Onderdonk's 1880s railway construction crews, the most difficult stretch was from Yale to Spuzzum. Tunnels, the bane of the railway contractor, were the only solution to the problem of rock outcrops that dipped their toes in the river. Within 1 mile (1.6 km) of Yale, four tunnels had to be blasted. Scarcely 1.5 miles (2.4 km) farther along a second series of six tunnels were needed, and three more required to complete the access to Spuzzum. At places, men were often lowered 200 ft. (60 m) down a sheer cliff in order to set powder blasts. It was inevitable that many accidents happened.

Typical was one on May 27, 1880. Three blasting shots were set at the east end of No. 1 tunnel. When triggered, it seemed that all three exploded simultaneously and workmen moved back to clear the debris. Just as William Flynn and two others reached the tunnel mouth, another explosion occurred, seriously injuring all three. The other two recovered but Flynn died — one of thirty-two men killed on the first 19 miles (30.4 km) of construction.

**Blasting Powder Factory:** Construction of the CPR through the rock walls of the Fraser Canyon required tons of blasting powder. Since the cost and danger of freighting it in proved prohibitive, Onderdonk started to make his own. A few miles (kilometers) beyond Emory Creek, a factory was erected and, complete with a maze of bins, tanks, immense jars, and sixteen men, turned out 1,200 lbs. (544 kg) a day.

Vancouver 106.6 (171.7 km) — Kamloops 161.4 (259.8 km)
**Emory Creek Provincial Park:** Contains 34 campsites and a picnicking area in a secluded location on the site of Emory City. It also has a Stop of Interest historical plaque:

EARLY CHINESE: "With the first wave of impetuous gold seekers in 1858, the Chinese came to B.C. Following the roving white miners, these industrious and patient people gleaned the gold that others failed to mine. With baskets and hand tools they helped to build the Cariboo Road, then later our railroads. They remained, becoming honoured and valuable citizens."

**River Fishing:** While the silt-laden Fraser River itself doesn't offer much opportunity, fishing is often quite productive at creek mouths such as Emory. "Jack" salmon — precocious two-year-old spring salmon which can weigh up to 3 lbs. (1.3 kg) — bite spinners and other lures. Consult the fishing regulations, however, since all salmon over 20 inches (50 cm) must be released. The run starts in May, peaking in July and August.

Vancouver 110.3 (177.6 km) — Kamloops 157.7 (253.9 km)
**Yale:** At the southern approach to this historic community are two Stop of Interest plaques:

THE YALE CONVENTION — "By 1868, the gold rushes that had founded British Columbia were over, the public debt was soaring and many were dissatisfied with the colonial government. On September 14, 1868, 26 delegates from all over the colony met at Yale for a convention of the Confederation League. This convention did much to stimulate popular support for the idea of union with Canada as a solution to the colony's problems."

HISTORIC YALE: "This was the head of navigation on the Fraser River. Founded in 1848 as a Hudson's Bay Company fur post, Fort Yale later became a roaring gold-rush town and for 20 years was the starting point of the famous Cariboo Wagon Road. Yale faded with the gold-rush but boomed again in C.P.R construction days as a wide open western town."

Travellers passing through this community with its tree-lined streets and peaceful setting on the bank of the Fraser River little realize that it once hummed with the activity of a city long before either New Westminster or Vancouver were born.

Named after Fort Langley commander James ("Little") Yale, it was established in 1848 while a new fur-trade route to the Interior was being investigated. At the height of the 1858 gold rush, at least 3,000 miners were working gravel bars on the 15 miles (24 km) of river between Hope and Yale. It isn't difficult to imagine that with some of these bars yielding hundreds of thousands of dollars in an era when the average wage was a few cents an hour, Yale was a riotous place. Saloons and dance halls numbered in the scores and pokes of gold were common tender. Seventy thousand dollars passed over the bar of one saloon in a three-week period.

New gold discoveries were being made almost hourly and the prospectors didn't have to go very far. Mr. Hinks, the Gold Commissioner at Yale, wrote: "Some miners commenced sinking a shaft near the Indian house this side of Fort Yale Creek and discovered good diggings of coarse gold. I was, however, compelled to stop further progress, otherwise Fort Yale Town would not exist; much disappointment was manifested by my interference."

Until 1861 when construction started on the Cariboo Wagon Road, all traffic northward was by foot or mule train over a circuitous trail leading to Kamloops. Yale witnessed the colorful spectacle of thousands of pack-toting miners and loaded mules wending their way out of town. From the completion of the Cariboo Road in 1863 until 1884 when the CPR virtually destroyed the road, Yale remained the lower terminus of that wild spectacular route. From its pioneer depots started the swaying coaches, covered wagons, traction engines, plodding oxen, and heavily burdened mules.

In this rough setting it seems almost incongruous that Yale should become the site of a Canadian girls' boarding school. In 1879 the Anglican Sisters of that Order from Norfolk, England, founded such a school with an enrollment of fifty. The fee for entrance was $5, with board and education $30 a month. Piano and violin instruction was an additional $5 a month, as were lessons in painting. Unfortunately, the once beautifully landscaped grounds and the old school have disappeared.

LOCAL PLACES AND NOTES OF INTEREST:
**Visitor Information:** During summer the Tourist Bureau on the south side of the Highway in Yale is open.

Since the gold rush of 1858 Yale has been the "Gateway to the Fraser Canyon." One of its links to the past is St. John's Church, built in 1860 and still in use.

**Historic Yale Museum:** One block off the Highway on Douglas Street in a park-like setting, this interesting museum has a slide show, an excellent display of photographs and newspaper clippings and other material which portrays the 1858 gold rush, the Cariboo Wagon Road era, railway construction and other aspects of a colorful past. On the grounds is a monument to the Chinese railway workers:

CHINESE CONSTRUCTION WORKERS ON THE PACIFIC RAILWAY: "In the early 1880's contractor Andrew Onderdonk brought thousands of labourers from China to help build Pacific Railway through the mountains of British Columbia. About three-quarters of the men who worked on the section between the Pacific and Craigellachie were Chinese. Although considered excellent workers they received one dollar a day, half the pay of a white worker. Hundreds of Chinese died from accidents or illness for the work was dangerous and living conditions poor. Those who remained in Canada when the railway was completed securely established the basis of British Columbia's Chinese community."

**St. John the Divine Anglican Church:** On the corner of Douglas Street near the museum, St. John's is the oldest church on the B.C. Mainland still on its original site. Built in 1860 by the Royal Engineers, the church was a landmark for the thousands of miners and others who ventured to the Cariboo. As it approached the century mark, however, the building faced demolition. Fortunately, donations from across Canada provided funds for emergency repairs. Then the late R. C. Gibbs, a Vancouver fishing tackle manufacturer, donated money for a complete renovation which included new lighting, floor and a pulpit — a detail that the original builders had overlooked.

Regular services are still held in the historic church with visitors welcome any day of the week. The bell which tolls on Sunday is the same one donated by well-wishers in England and shipped via Cape Horn over 125 years ago. The church is shaded by a magnificent English oak which may be another link to the past. Story has it that the acorn was brought from England and planted in 1860 when the church was being constructed.

**Cariboo Wagon Road and Barnard's Express:** On the river bank at the corner of Front and Albert Streets are a commemorative cairn and an historical display panel:

CARIBOO WAGON ROAD: "Constructed between 1862 and 1865 . . . the 400-mile Cariboo Road was the best and most used of several routes into the Cariboo gold fields. Until 1885 the road began at Yale, the head of steam navigation on the Fraser and aimed to secure all trade for that river, thus excluding American competition. Intended to reduce the cost of goods in the mining area, and to encourage British immigrants and capitalists to come there, the road put the Colony deeply into debt."

BARNARD'S EXPRESS AND STAGE LINE 1860-1885: "At first Barnard carried letters on foot between Yale and Cariboo, a distance of 380 miles. Later he used ponies, and when the Wagon Road was completed, in stagecoaches. Barnard's express, known as the BX, operated the longest stagecoach run in North America.

"Highly respected, Barnard served as MLA for Yale district. In 1886, the BX changed headquarters from Yale to Ashcroft, and was renamed B.C. Express Co. The line was bought in 1894 by Steve Tingley, a veteran stagecoach driver and operated until Oct. 1915.''

The express office was located on the corner of Albert and Front Streets, for over two decades the best known address in the Interior. From here until the early 1880s when CPR construction destroyed the Cariboo Wagon Road, stagecoaches and canvas-topped freight wagons left on their 400-mile (644-km) journey to the Cariboo goldfields. In 1864 alone the stagecoaches travelled 110,600 miles (178,065 km), and carried nearly $5 million in treasure and valuables. Most of the treasure was gold — at today's price worth some $150 million.

**Hill's Bar:** About 1 mile (1.6 km) south of Yale on the east bank of the Fraser, this patch of gravel was the site of the first gold discovery in the spring of 1858. It resulted in the rush which in the next few months sent upwards of 30,000 men stampeding to the river. As the Reverend Lundin summarized: ''. . . never in the migrations of men has been seen a rush so sudden and vast.''

James Moore, one of the original discoverers, later recalled: ''. . . we left Hope and camped on a bar at noon to cook lunch. While doing so, one of our party noticed particles of gold in the moss that was growing on the rocks. On the bar he washed a pan of that moss and got a prospect. After lunch we all prospected and found good pay dirt. We named the bar 'Hill's' after the man who got the first prospect.''

Thus by accident was discovered what proved to be the Fraser River's richest bar. By 1875 it had yielded an estimated $2 million from an area equivalent to a few city blocks. On one occasion two partners took out 46 lbs. (21 kg) of gold between December 1858 and April 1859.

**Whiskey and Indians:** The bonanza that was Hill's Bar quickly collected opportunists. One such man was the captain of a small ship that plied the river to Yale. Taking advantage of the Indians working on Hill's Bar, he arrived with a boat load of whiskey. By selling it at $5 a bottle, he envisioned passing his old age in considerable splendor.

The outnumbered whites, fearful of the consequences from a drunken Indian mob, offered to buy the whole cargo. The captain refused. The apprehensive whites took matters into their own hands and boarded the boat. The whiskey was poured into the river and the thoroughly frightened captain given one hour to make himself and his boat scarce.

**Bloody Edwards:** A picturesque character at Hill's Bar was an Englishman known as ''Bloody Edwards.'' Being the only Englishman among the rowdy collection of American miners, he was the object of much horseplay. After the frequent celebrations, Edwards was alternately threatened and cajoled into becoming an American citizen. His answer was always the same — he was quite content to be ''a bloody good Englishman.'' To positively finish the argument, he would then lead the miners in giving ''three bloody good cheers for the Queen.''

Since Edwards was proprietor of a store that stocked whiskey as a necessity of wilderness life, he had lots of company. One evening the conversation was about bravery and it wasn't long before someone questioned the courage of "the bloody Englishman." Edwards quickly responded. Taking a burning candle to the unlighted back of the store, he held it at arm's length and asked the men to shoot it out. Fortunately, one sober individual realized the possible tragic outcome and diffused the confrontation by calling for drinks for everyone.

**Yale Waterfront:** For the first quarter century of Yale's life its main street fronted the Fraser since the river was its highway. During the navigation season flat-bottomed sternwheel steamers called regularly, their mooring rings still embedded in the rocks.

The first sternwheeler to ply the Fraser River was the *Umatilla,* which arrived at Victoria from the Columbia River on July 13, 1858. On the Columbia she had the misfortune to plummet over a rapids on her maiden voyage, killing a passenger. On the Fraser, however, she was more fortunate. Besides being the first sternwheeler on the river, she was first to explore Harrison River and Lake and first to reach Yale. When she arrived at the upriver community on July 21 an eyewitness wrote:

"The town was thrown into a high state of excitement, upon hearing the screeching of a steam-whistle, and a rumor gaining circulation that a little sternwheeler was on her way up the river. Everybody was soon on the lookout . . . and canoes were sent beyond the bend of the river . . . to ascertain the truth of the report. Soon we learned by the shoutings along the banks of the river and the continuous discharge of guns and pistols, that the report was true; whereupon, there was the greatest rejoicing and pleasure manifested by everyone, and powder was burnt amidst the wildest excitement . . . ."

While the gold-rush vessels would prove profitable for their owners, they weren't exactly built for comfort. A passenger on the *Umatilla,* an Austrian professor named Dr. Carl Friesach, later wrote: ". . . the boat did not contain any cabins and even mattresses and blankets were lacking; the floor of the saloon was so covered with coal dust that it was impossible to lie down without getting very dirty. Moreover the passengers, who were mostly miners, were so numerous that it was difficult to find sleeping room. Finally two of us lay down on the dining room table, another under it . . . ."

When they passed the mountains near present day Chilliwack they ". . . were prevented from enjoying the beautiful landscape by a strong wind, which, blowing in the direction of our course, caused the sparks from the smokestack to fall all about us, burning holes in our hats and clothes."

In addition to offering spartan comfort for their passengers, the sternwheel owners frequently formed a monopoly to keep freight rates high. To combat this price fixing, in 1860 a group of Yale businessmen built their own sternwheeler. She cost $31,000 and was appropriately called the *Fort Yale.* But as related in Heritage House book, *Paddlewheels on the Frontier — The Story of B.C.-Yukon Sternwheel Steamers,* her career was brief and tragic:

"She arrived at Yale on her maiden voyage on November 26, 1860. She was received . . . with every manifestation of rejoicing . . . Cannons and anvils were fired, and British and American flags hoisted . . . a dinner was held, and the dancing continued till an early hour in the morning.

"She made the return trip to New Westminster in 7½ hours, a new

From the early 1860s until construction of the CPR in the 1880s destroyed the Cariboo Wagon Road, Yale was the supply point for much of Interior B.C.
The photos show Yale in 1868 with a sternwheel steamer at the landing, and oxen-drawn freight wagons and a stagecoach ready to leave for Barkerville some 400 miles (640 km) to the north.

record. On December 26 she set another record, one most welcome to lonely bachelors. Among her passengers was the first single white woman to arrive at Yale. A few months later, the *Fort Yale* was again in the news, although for a most tragic reason.

"On April 14, at Union Bar some two miles above Hope, she blew up. So great was the blast that a 90-pound chunk of boiler was blown a quarter mile inland. 'TERRIBLE CATASTROPHE' said a headline in the *Victoria Colonist* at Victoria, where flags were lowered to half mast.

"An eye-witness account was given by a passenger, H. Lee Alley: 'The noise resembled, together with the crash, a heavy blow upon a sharp-sounding Chinese gong. The cabin floor raised and then fell in; at the same time the hurricane roof fell upon us, cutting our heads more or less, and blocking up all means of escape forward of the dinner table. We quickly made for the windows and doors in the after-part of the cabin, and got on the roof of the hurricane house, and there beheld a scene that baffles all description, and such as I trust I may never witness again. The boat, but a few seconds before nobly bucking against the swift current, was now a sinking mass of ruins from stem to stern — scarcely anything remained in sight above water, but a small portion of her bow and the after part of her saloon, and those gradually disappearing below water. Five or six human beings, their faces streaming with blood, and presenting an awful appearance, were struggling for life.'

"The shattered vessel was swept below Hope where survivors were rescued. Five white men, including her captain, Smith Jamieson, and an unknown number of Indians and Chinese died in the wreck. Among survivors was James Ellison. He had been in the pilothouse with Captain Jamieson, and since the pilothouse was almost directly over the boiler, it received the full force of the blast. Ellison was blown high in the air but landed in the water with only bruises. Another passenger, Samuel Powers, wasn't so fortunate. He was also blown high in the air, but landed on shore and was killed. No trace was ever found of 26-year-old Captain Jamieson.''

**Pioneer Cemetery and Edward Stout:** Located on the south side of the Trans-Canada Highway about 1 mile (1.6 km) south of Yale, this is one of B.C.'s oldest cemeteries. Headboards date back to 1863, with Edward Stout, one of the Cariboo gold rush's best known miners, among those buried.

Stout arrived at Fort Yale on May 20, 1858, and joined a party of twenty-four miners. As they struggled up the Fraser Canyon, they did not know that the Indians, resenting the white intrusion, were murdering any miners they saw. Scores were killed, their heads cut off and bodies tossed into the river. When Stout and his companions reached Nicomen Creek some 60 miles (96.6 km) above Yale they were warned by a friendly squaw about the warfare. They immediately retreated toward Fort Yale and reached Jackass Mountain in safety. But here the Indians attacked, using arrows poisoned with rattlesnake venom. Three men, including their leader, were wounded and died in agony next day.

The survivors continued their retreat, harassed by the Indians. In one battle the miners killed twenty-two but lost six. When they finally reached China Bar some 20 miles (32 km) above Fort Yale only five were alive, all wounded and too weak to move. Stout had been hit by seven arrows and lived only because the Indians were out of poison. As the despairing men lay behind a pile of stones waiting for the final attack and certain death, they heard gunfire. Armed miners were moving upstream, a show of force which quickly brought peace.

Once Stout recovered he again headed up the Fraser. In the Cariboo Mountains some 400 miles (644 km) to the north he was a member of the party which discovered Williams Creek, the richest of all the creeks that yielded $1,000 a foot (25 cm). Stout's Gulch, just upstream from Barkerville, commemorates him. After his mining days he settled in Yale where he died in 1924. He was ninety-nine, proud that never once had he smoked or drunk liquor.

**Spirit Cave Hiking Trail:** The trail starts opposite the cemetery. For fitness buffs the hike to the caves near the top of the mountain takes about an hour. From the summit is a breathtaking view of the Fraser Canyon entrance and the Cascade Mountains on the east side of the river.

The significance of this cave in the lives of the early Indians has been largely lost, but it is known that they used it as a look-out. Steep bluffs below the opening limit access from that direction, so the Indians reached it by ropes from above.

**Douglas Portage, or Brigade Trail:** At Yale Creek near the northern outskirts of Yale, the white man's first trail started up the Fraser Canyon. It climbed the small draw below the steep mountain side and then ran parallel to the river several miles (kilometers) back.

Among those buried at Yale's Pioneer Cemetery is Edward "Ned" Stout, one of the best known of some 30,000 miners who stampeded to the Fraser River in 1858.

The establishment of the 49th parallel as the International Boundary cut off the Columbia River route to the Interior and made necessary a new route from the Lower Mainland to the Interior. In 1847, Chief Factor James Douglas and "Little" Yale, confronted with the terrifying gorge north of Fort Yale, sought and found back from the river a mountain defile that offered a rough but possible route to what is today Spuzzum.

**Original Wagon Road:** Just across Yale Creek a road leaves the Highway and crosses the railway tracks. It is part of the original Cariboo Wagon Road but only about a mile (1.6 km) is open. This short section, however, graphically illustrates the horrendous task that confronted road builders with their picks, shovels and gunpowder over 125 years ago. At the entrance to the Canyon, a wall of rock rises almost from the bank of the rapid-torn river, although here the engineers were fortunate since there was a small area of flat ground. Elsewhere, as old photos show, they had to hang the road over gorges on wood cribbing, and even blast it into rocks.

**Lady Franklin Rock:** At the mouth of the Canyon where the original road ends is a massive black rock, the water swirling angrily round its base. This treacherous conspiracy of water and stone symbolizes the terrors of the rocky gorge for anyone foolhardy enough to attempt access by water.

The naming of this rock resulted from a series of events. In 1845, the noted Arctic explorer Sir John Franklin was placed in command of an expedition to survey the waters and coasts from Baffin's Bay westward. His group was last heard of on July 26, 1845. Thirty-nine relief expeditions were sent to search for him and his companions, but all failed. In 1859, Lady

F.J. Barnard, above, founded the B.X. stagecoach company.

Steve Tingley began as a driver for the B.X. Company and eventually bought the firm.

Lady Franklin visited Yale in 1861 and is commemorated by Lady Franklin Rock in the Fraser River.

Franklin in desperation purchased and outfitted the *Fox* for one last search. She had already financed three unsuccessful searches, but this time Captain F. McClintock of the *Fox* brought back some news. He learned that Franklin had died of natural causes on June 11, 1847, but could find nothing about the fate of the other 128 men and Franklin's ships, HMS *Erebus* and *Terror*. Not until 1880 were remains of the expedition found on King William Island, just off Canada's Arctic coast. The two ships had been trapped in the ice sometime after July 1845 and their crews attempted to escape by land. All 128 died of sickness or starvation. Over 100 years later in 1984, scientists opened the shallow grave of one of the sailors. His body was perfectly preserved in its grave of ice.

After receiving definite news that her husband was dead, Lady Franklin, although sixty-eight and frail, embarked on a world tour that included Yale. Her niece, Sophia Cracroft, accompanied her and left the following account of a canoe journey up a few miles of the Fraser on March 9, 1861:

"It had been arranged the evening before, that we were to be taken up the river in a canoe through a fine pass known only by the Spanish term of Canon (pronounced Canyon) up to some Falls. . . . At 10 o'clock one of the largest canoes was waiting for us, which on entering, we found to be manned by 12 Indians, all dressed in red woollen shirts, with gay ribbons in their caps, in honor of my Aunt. They rowed of course in the Indian fashion, with short paddles, 5 at one end, 5 at the other, with one man standing in the bow, the other at the stern — we seated in the middle. They make very quick, short strokes which send the canoe on very rapidly unless the current be very strong against them which it was, in going *up* the river, so that, tho' they began to sing a sort of chorus, they soon stopped it, all their exertion being required for the paddles. The current & eddies were so strong that we repeatedly had to shoot directly across the river in order to find still water, and 3 times the rowers had to jump ashore and drag the canoe through the rapid stream . . . .

"After a pull of nearly 5 miles against the stream, past several mining parties who were sluicing (or fluming) with good results, we came to the Falls which though of little height, yet stretch entirely across the stream & render it necessary to carry the canoes past them, by land. An American has constructed 'ways' upon the bank, on which runs a platform bearing a canoe which is dragged up on it, and slides off into the water at the other end. A very large canoe heavily laden with freight for the upper mining country passed and we landed & stopped to see the transit.

"The canoe was entirely emptied of its load, chiefly in the form of small casks, & bags & bales — they were filled with coffee, flour, tea, rice, (the last in matted parcels just as it comes from China) butter, nails &c &c ad infinitum. The canoe was then hauled out of the water upon the platform, by the Indians, about 20 in number under a man called 'long Jack' from his great size whose vocation is that of carrying freight up the country — this is called 'packing' and he is 'a packer', — the trade is a highly profitable one, the charges being enormous. After the canoe has been carried above the Fall, the freight is carried after it, also on the platform.

"We pulled back easily, the current carrying us down with great rapidity, and our boatmen began again to sing in chorus, or rather one gave a sort of recitative (which we were told set forth the charms of their vocation) echoed in chorus by the rest, whose lungs seem to be in excellent order. On reaching the narrowest part of the Canon, we beheld (suspended from the rafters of a salmon drying shed) a long pole stretching over the stream, on which was hung a white banner with the words 'Lady Franklin Pass' printed in large letters. The Indians stopped their paddling and we were told that this name was bestowed by the inhabitants of Yale in honor of my Aunt's visit, the said inscription being saluted from the opposite bank, by dipping a flag (the Union Jack) 3 times . . . .''

NOW RESUMES ROUTE DESCRIPTION OF THE TRANS-CANADA HIGHWAY:

Vancouver 111.1 (178.9 km) — Kamloops 156.9 (252.6 km)

**Yale Tunnel:** This was the last of seven tunnels built between here and Boston Bar during the 1960s reconstruction of the Highway.

**Abandonment of the Cariboo Wagon Road:** After the completion of this famous road it served for almost twenty years before being abandoned as the main transportation link between the rich northern goldfields and the Coast.

During the early 1880s the gigantic task of building the CPR through the Canyon caused great damage to the wagon road. Crossings were numerous and often the cuts or fills for the railway grade jeopardized the road. Detours were frequent — and dangerous. On March 3, 1881, a stage with veteran driver Alexander Tingley at the reins plunged over a cliff below Spuzzum. Two passengers suffered broken limbs and two horses were killed.

Two months later, Tingley tried to work his way past a fall of rock caused by blasting, but caught the front wheel of his four-horse stage on a rock and toppled over. A CPR workman saw what was happening and tried to stop the coach from going over by putting his shoulder against it. He was flung over the embankment and struck a tree which prevented him from dropping into the river. The near disaster averted, railway men righted the coach, dusted off the passengers and sent the stage on its way. The workman was only slightly injured.

As the railway was completed towards Kamloops, headquarters for the stagecoaches and freight wagons heading for Cariboo gradually moved northward. Finally, in 1886 a new community called Ashcroft on the CPR became the starting point for passengers and freight bound for the Cariboo and Central B.C.

Gradually, the historic old road fell into disrepair and its almost total abandonment was hastened by the great flood of 1894 which washed away much of the trestle work used in skirting the cliffs and bluffs. Then, until 1915 and the advent of the CNR, the CPR was the sole means of transportation.

**Construction of the first Fraser Canyon Highway:** With the increasing use of the automobile after World War One, it was apparent that a road was again needed up the great gorge. With two railways already notched into the rocky walls and taking full advantage of whatever low terraces there were, finding a route was difficult. Surveying started in 1920 and construction four years later. The highway was completed to Lytton in 1926 and to Ashcroft the following year.

**Construction of today's Highway:** Between 1950-60 the Federal and ten Provincial governments entered into agreements to upgrade existing highways or build new stretches of the Trans-Canada Highway from Victoria on the Pacific Coast to Newfoundland on the Atlantic, nearly 5,000 miles (8,050 km). The Highway was to have a 100-ft. (30-m) right-of-way with pavement 24 ft. (7.3 m) wide and 10-ft. (3-m) gravel shoulders where feasible. While these standards were easy to meet over most of the route, the Fraser Canyon was a notable exception. Even with modern equipment, in some areas it was impossible to build the Highway to a uniform width because it was sandwiched between the railway and the river. When the Trans-Canada project was finally completed, it not only gave Canada its first national highway but also the longest paved one in the world. The project cost over $1 billion.

By contrast, the original Cariboo Wagon Road from Yale to Barkerville, some 400 miles (644 km), was about $1 million. Given today's costs, however, both the Cariboo Wagon Road and the Trans-Canada Highway were bargains. The Coquihalla Highway completed between Hope and Merritt in 1986 cost $250 million — for only 70 miles (113 km). One snowshed alone cost $5 million.

Vancouver 112.7 (181.5 km) — Kamloops 155.3 (250 km)

**Stop of Interest:** CARIBOO WAGON ROAD: "It was one of the most difficult construction jobs in the British Empire, but the colony needed this road to the Cariboo goldfields. From 1861 to 1863 the small body of Royal Engineers sent from England surveyed and supervised the construction of this 400-mile road. Their motto 'Whither Right and Glory Lead'."

**The Royal Engineers:** Much of the early pattern of culture and development in British Columbia was laid by this famous group of men. In 1858, the scattered white population of the mainland did not number over 150. Then, with the sensational rumors of rich goldfields reaching California, tens of thousands of opportunists trekked northward to flood the country. To maintain order and "to develop institutes of civilization," the Secretary for Colonies, Sir Edward Bulwer Lytton, sent 150 highly trained and carefully selected specialists from England.

After several minor changes in location, they established a permanent camp at Sapperton at New Westminster. For the next five years until their disbanding in 1863, these engineers accomplished a prodigious amount of work. The primary road systems of the Lower Mainland were surveyed and the first official maps prepared. Aside from the surveying and construction aspects, they designed the first schools and churches, the first coat of arms and first postage stamp. Their collection of books started the first public library, they surveyed the original townsites of communities that include New Westminster, Lytton, Lillooet and Quesnel, and even built the first 15 miles (24 km) of what became the Hope-Princeton Highway. Although a list of their accomplishments fills a book, the 6 miles (9.6 km) of the Cariboo Wagon Road through the first part of the Fraser Canyon was their most difficult and hazardous project.

Yale and the Cariboo Wagon Road in 1868. Unlike modern engineers who bored through the rock bluff at the entrance to the Canyon, the Royal Engineers in 1863 had to suspend the road over the river on piles, wooden bridges and rock cribbing.

**The Cariboo Wagon Road:** In 1861 Governor Douglas outlined a plan as bold and imaginative as anything previously undertaken in North America. It called for construction of an 18-ft. (5.4-m) wagon road north 400 miles (644 km) through the rock barrier of the Fraser Canyon and across the lonely wilderness to the goldfields. Considering that the permanent population of the colony was under 7,000, the project was a stupendous undertaking.

As a start, in October 1861 the Royal Engineers were ordered to survey a route from Yale through the canyon to Cook's Ferry (Spences Bridge). The same month a contract was let for construction of the section between Boston Bar and Lytton. The first 6 miles (9.6 km) northward from Fort Yale had to be blasted from the face of the cliffs, with some sections built right over the river on stilts and cribbing. In May 1862 the Royal Engineers started this section. Other parts of the canyon were let to private contractors, most prominent of whom were J. W. Trutch and Thomas Spence. Meanwhile to the north, G. B. Wright had completed the Lillooet-Clinton section and was awarded another contract from Clinton 130 miles (209 km) to Soda Creek.

Work on all sections progressed steadily. By September 1863 the road was completed from Yale northward nearly 300 miles (483 km) to Soda Creek. Here a sternwheel steamer was built to ply the Fraser River to Quesnel where a trail headed 55 miles (88 km) eastward to Barkerville. Then in 1864, G. B. Wright was given a contract to complete a wagon road from Quesnel to Barkerville which was finished the next year. Thus there are actually two completion dates — the original section was finished in 1863 and the Barkerville extension in 1865.

Vancouver 113.7 (183 km) — Kamloops 154.3 (248.5 km)
**Saddle Rock Tunnel,** named after an immense white rock which is shaped like a saddle and splits the river into two channels.

**The Yale Midden:** As mentioned at Mile 33.6, the Indians have been fishing the Lower Fraser River for some 9,000 years. The reason that archeologists are fairly certain of this time period is the midden discovered by August Milliken about 2 miles (3.2 km) upstream from Yale. The site was excavated to 26 ft. (8 m) which spanned an exposure of some 9,000 years. (This time span was determined by radiocarbon dating and comparing data with excavations at The Dalles on the Columbia River where Dr. L. Cressman from the University of Oregon collected some 200,000 salmon vertebrae from deposits of about the same age. The fascinating archeological detective story is contained in a booklet called *The Fraser's History,* published by the Burnaby Historical Society.)

**Indian Fishing:** The fishing grounds along the Fraser River from Yale to Hells Gate were regarded as the best in B.C. and every summer Indians gathered to catch the salmon which provided the bulk of their winter food. Sockeye were — and remain — the most abundant, although spring salmon and steelhead at 30 lbs. (13.6 kg) and over were (and still are) frequently taken. (Visitors should remember that it is illegal to buy these fish from the Indians.)

Some of the Indians still prepare the fish in the same manner witnessed by Simon Fraser in 1808. First, the head is cut off and the fish cleaned.

Then the backbone is split from the flesh down to the tail, but not separated. The fish is spread flat and slit into strips which dry faster and more uniformly than a solid piece. Sharpened twigs are then threaded through the flesh to keep it flat while drying. Finally, the fish is hung on a pole for three weeks to dry in the sun and wind.

**Indian Cemeteries:** Before the white man disrupted the Indian's life style, there were many Indian villages on both sides of the river, with cemeteries that were thousands of years old. Burials were made in large cedar boxes into which numerous bodies were placed. Sometimes the dead were wrapped in cedar-bark mats and put in the box in a sitting position. The boxes were then set on poles or staging. After the missionaries came to B.C., the old cedar boxes were removed and their contents buried, the last grave-box being thus treated in 1898.

**Keekwilee Holes:** Unlike the Coastal Indians who lived in massive cedar houses, or the Plains Indians in their hide tipis, the Indian in the Lower Fraser drainage and a few other Interior locations lived in holes in the ground in winter. There are various spellings of the word, including kikili, kekuli, kikwilly, and keekwillee, but regardless of spelling nowhere else in North America did Indians live in this type of dwelling.

The houses were always near water and inhabited by groups of related families. There were seldom more than three or four dwellings in a group and often only one. Sometimes up to thirty people lived under one roof. Hammocks took the place of beds and cedar-bark mats on the floor were used as tables.

When a keekwilee was required, a site with loose soil was selected and often a "raising bee" organized so that the building was sometimes completed in a day. The first part of construction was marking the circumference. Then the women dug out the soil with their digging sticks and wooden scrapers. The loose earth was put into large baskets and dumped near the hole to be used for covering the keekwilee's sloping sides. After trees had been cut, barked, and hauled with bark ropes to the building site, four sturdy upright posts were planted in the ground and notched at the top to support four heavy sloping rafters. Secondary rafters were leaned against the main rafters, giving a rough conical effect. Then horizontal poles about 2 ft. (60 cm) apart were tied to the rafters and formed the support for the roof covering. This framework was covered with poles and pieces of split wood from the ground to an entrance hole at the top. The framework was then covered with pine needles or grass and layered with earth.

Because of heavy rainfall, the Lower Thompson and Coast Salish Indians lined their houses with big pieces of cedar bark. A large, notched log placed almost upright to the top entrance served as a ladder. The last of these houses was abandoned in the 1890s.

Vancouver 115.4 (185.8 km) — Kamloops 152.6 (245.7 km)
**Sawmill Creek and Bridge:** The original Cariboo Wagon Road and then the first Fraser Canyon Highway were near the creek mouth where depressions marked the site of three keekwilee houses. Two were quite large, being at least 20 ft. (6 m) across.

A twelve-horse outfit on the Cariboo Wagon Road during construction of the CPR in the 1880s. The railway destroyed much of the pioneer road, cutting vehicle traffic between Yale and Ashcroft until the Fraser Canyon Highway, opposite page, was completed in 1926.

Vancouver 117.8 (189.7 km) — Kamloops 150.2 (241.8 km)

**Sailor Bar Tunnel and the luck of Old 97:** In the pioneer era of railroading in the Canyon no other train attracted history like Old No. 97 (no connection to the song of the same name). On the night of May 8, 1906, she was held up between Kamloops and Monte Creek by Bill Miner, Shorty Dunn and Louis Colquhoun. She later got revenge when Miner and his companions were convicted and she transported them from Kamloops to the penitentiary at New Westminster to serve long sentences. (See Heritage House book, *Bill Miner . . . STAGECOACH & TRAIN ROBBER.*)

In the early morning of January 15, 1909, No. 97 was Vancouver-bound through a snowstorm when she again wrote her name into the historical record. With engineer Clifford Carscadden at the throttle of lead engine

496, followed by James Foster in 841, the celebrated passenger train wedged its way through the falling snow near Saddle Rock. One-half mile (.8 km) north of Sailor Bar Bluff siding they noticed a slide across the track. Thinking that it was only snow, they increased speed with the intent of ramming their way through. The train hit the obstruction at an estimated 40 miles (64 km) an hour.

No powder-puff of snow, it was a 50-ft. (15-m) slide, packed with ice, trees and rock, and yielded not an inch. The lead engine mounted the slide, turned almost at right angles and slid towards the river 100 ft. (30 m) below. Fireman H. Finney felt the engine lift and jumped safely. Then occurred an event that could have killed many people. For twenty-five years, CPR engines had been jumping the rails on the dangerous Canyon run. Every time, however, the couplings between engine and passenger cars had snapped in time to prevent the heavy locomotives from dragging passenger cars down embankments. This night was different.

Couplings failed to snap and engine 841 followed its leader down the embankment. Engineer Foster stayed in his seat and was scalded to death, but fireman S. F. Cranston leapt out half way down the slope. The mail car, baggage car and tourist coach hurtled after 841.

By coincidence, among the passengers was B.C. Police Constable William Fernie who had played a major role in capturing Bill Miner and his companions. "My coach gave a lurch forward and seemed to be completely turned over," he later recalled. "The car was well filled and women screamed in terror. It seemed an age before the car stopped. Even after lodging on its side, it slipped quite a distance through the snow and ice towards the river which we knew was terribly near."

When the dazed passengers managed to scramble through the shattered windows of the coach, they saw that both engines barely protruded from the water. The upended mail car was 40 ft. (12 m) out in the river but the mail clerks were able to scramble through its rear door and safely to shore. The express car also lay in the water. Above them, a quarter way down the embankment, the first class coach had come to a stop.

Though thirty of the passengers and the fireman, baggage men and mail clerks were injured, only the two engineers lost their lives. Had the tourist and first class coaches plunged into the river, all on board probably would have died.

Five months later in June, No. 97 was back in the news when she was again held up at Monte Creek. The first thought that crossed police minds was that Bill Miner — who had escaped from the penitentiary in 1907 — was involved, but it quickly became apparent that this was the work of a new three-man gang. Although 100 men scoured the area between Savona and Ashcroft to where Constable Fernie had traced the hold-up men, there was no sign of them until the afternoon of June 29. Then a CPR section foreman noticed three men in a boat drifting down the Thompson towards Ashcroft and gave the alarm.

Special Constable Isaac Decker, a crack shot, was stationed at the Ashcroft Bridge. Early in the evening he saw a boat approaching. There were only two men in it but they matched the descriptions of the wanted men. Cradling an army rifle, Decker went down to the bank. In the ensuing gun battle, Decker killed Dave Haney who proved to be the leader of the train robbers, but was knocked over by Haney's simultaneous shot. As Decker lay on the ground, the second bandit — believed to be Bill Haney — wounded him with a second blast. Several citizens ran to help, but the bandit, threatening them with a revolver and a shotgun, scrambled up the bank and disappeared. Constable Decker died that night. The identity of the third man was never discovered, nor was Bill Haney ever captured.

Vancouver 120.1 (193.4 km) — Kamloops 147.9 (238.1 km)
**Spuzzum Creek and Bridge:** On the delta of the creek is an old Indian village which contains the oldest consecrated Indian cemetery in B.C. In 1898, miners digging gold by the mouth of Spuzzum Creek accidentally struck a prehistoric burial ground. From 6-15 ft. (2-6.75 m) below the surface, about twenty skeletons were dug out. All had been interred in a sitting position around the remains of a large lodge fire.

**The Brigade Trail**, which started at Yale and was in use over 125 years ago, eased its way down the south side of Spuzzum Creek Canyon and then angled down the steep creek bank towards a ford. Unmistakable evidence of it remains as a short section of trail approaching the ford. Here the large boulders along the edge of the creek have been smoothed into a rough trail suitable for foot and horse travel.

Vancouver 121.6 (195.8 km) — Kamloops 146.4 (235.7 km)

**Spuzzum:** The first building was established here in 1848 to act as a depot for the Hudson's Bay Company brigade. For years it was simply known as Simon's House. Later the Indian name "Spozem" (little flat) was adapted to "Spuzzum."

Prior to the construction of the original Alexandra suspension bridge, a ferry crossed the Fraser River here, making its first run December 4, 1858. In later years Spuzzum was the site of a Cariboo Wagon Road toll station. Tolls were collected at Yale, Spuzzum, Lytton, Spences Bridge and Clinton, about five cents a pound (.454 kg) in all.

Vancouver 122.5 (197.2 km) — Kamloops 145.5 (234.3 km)

**Fraser River and Alexandra High Level Bridge:** This bridge crosses not only the Fraser but also the CPR and CNR tracks which are on both sides of the river. Overall length is 1,610 ft. (485 m), the center span is 805 ft. (242 m) and it is 130 ft. (40 m) above the river. At its completion it was the second largest fixed-arch span in the world — and may be still.

Upstream can be seen the graceful suspension bridge built in 1926 during the reconstruction of the Cariboo Wagon Road. It is virtually a duplicate of the original suspension bridge built by the Royal Engineers in 1863. The Royal Engineers' bridge cost $45,000, its modern counterpart was slightly more expensive — over $4 million.

**At the west end of the bridge** is an Historical Cairn and a Stop of Interest: J. W. TRUTCH, 1826-1904: "Construction of the Alexandra suspension bridge was the greatest achievement of one of British Columbia's first civil engineers, Joseph Trutch. Chief Commissioner of Lands and Works after 1864, he sat on the colony's Legislative Council. He led the delegation in 1870 which negotiated the terms of union with Canada and from 1871-76 served as the province's first lieutenant-governor."

**Historical Cairn:** "In commemoration of the work of Her Majesty's Royal Engineers and in respectful admiration of the skill and energy displayed by them from 1859 to 1863 in the construction of the original Cariboo Highway through the Fraser Canyon, this tablet is erected and dedicated."

**Railroad Rock Embankment:** Across the Highway from the Stop of Interest can be seen rockwork in a CPR retaining wall. Retaining walls were built from blocks of granite, some weighing over a ton (1 tonne) and fitted so exactly that joints are barely discernible. Since no mortar or cement was used, they can be truly called "dry walls." The granite was quarried across the river from Boston Bar by stonemasons from Scotland.

Vancouver 123 (198 km) — Kamloops 145 (233.5 km)

**Alexandra Bridge Provincial Park picnic ground** flanks both sides of the Highway on the east end of the bridge. Each site has rural toilets and picnic tables, and display panels which feature photos and text on the history

The suspension bridge at Alexandra in the early 1880s and, opposite, the first highway bridge opened in 1926. It is built on the site of the original 1863 bridge and is almost identical, although no longer in use.

of the area. The one on the east side of the highway is titled "CHOPPERS, GRADERS AND BLASTERS" and notes:

"In 1862 Joseph W. Trutch was awarded the contract for 11 miles above Alexandra, seven miles of which lay through sheer granite cliffs. A witness described the method of construction:

" 'There are three grades of men employed: choppers, who . . . cut down the trees . . . and fill up ravines with crib-work built of logs . . ., graders, who follow the choppers, with pick and shovel, grub out the stumps of the trees, and dig away or fill up the soil; and the blasters . . . who assault the rocks, where they are in the way, with drill and sledgehammers, and quickly demolish them afterwards with gunpowder'."

A letter from Trutch to Governor Douglas described the hazards confronting the road builders:

"Another cause of increased expenditure has arisen from the dangerous character of many portions of the work where the men have laboured in constant fear of their lives from the unexpectedly treacherous nature of rock under and amongst which they were working. In such circumstances the best men must devote a considerable portion of their time to looking after their own safety, and, in fact, can hardly be induced to work in such places at all. The China Bar Bluff was perhaps the worst point of this description. Here, when the road was nearly completed an immense slide of rock took place, extending 300 feet up the mountainside, carrying away or burying up all the work that had been done. A large party of men were employed for an entire month in repairing the injury done by this slide, and in bringing down all the loose rock from above what seemed at all likely to detach itself; and I have every confidence that this portion of the road is now sound and reliable. The difficulties encountered here however were much greater than I had reason to expect and have added very materially to the increased cost of the road. I am glad to be able to state in this connection that although many accidents have occurred to the workmen, six having been at one time thrown down and injured by a slide of rocks, only one life has been lost during the construction of the road."

The picnic site on the west side of the Highway has a kiosk with historical photos and captions, and illustrated panel, SALMON FISHING IN THE FRASER CANYON, with the following text:

"Salmon fishing has long been the major economic activity among Indian groups in the Fraser Canyon. Many varied methods of exploiting this important food resource have been developed during the 10,000-year history of this area.

"Traditional methods included the use of harpoons, dipnets and bag nets. The latter device was noted by the explorer Simon Fraser near Yale, in 1808: 'We observed the Indians fishing; their nets, which resembled purses, were fixed to the end of long poles and dragged between two canoes.'

"Dipnets, which are still in use, vary in size and are used from the riverbank. They are swept downstream through the current, lifted from the water and the process is repeated. Gill nets are a more recent development and involve the use of a net which is run out along a pole from the river bank by means of a line and pulley.

"Many of the fish are cut up, hung on rocks . . . and dried for later use.

"Salmon fishing remains an important subsistence activity in the area today."

At the north end of the picnic site is the road which gives access to the suspension bridge built in 1926. Although the road is closed to vehicles, a visit to the bridge can be completed in a leisurely half hour.

**The 1863 Alexandra Suspension Bridge:** This bridge was on the same site as its 1926 replacement. In 1863 after careful exploration, the Royal Engineers chose this river crossing as the most favorable. Considering the difficulties of the time, the bridge was justly hailed as an engineering marvel. The deck of the old bridge was about 10 ft. (3 m) lower than the 1926 one. During the flood of 1894 the river actually washed over a section of the deck.

On a bench above the east end of the bridge is the remnant of a very old building site. Pictures from the late 1860s show several neat white houses on this flat and a fenced-in orchard. A few fruit trees have survived, with a touch of long-ago nostalgia provided by an ancient lilac bush.

**Cariboo Wagon Road:** Old photographs show the original road swinging up-river from the eastern end of the bridge instead of climbing, as did the 1926 road, by means of two switchbacks. The start of the wagon road is noticeable some 20 ft. (6 m) past the end of the present bridge, and 10 ft. (3 m) lower. The 1863 road may be followed for a short distance along the mossy, tree-lined river bank.

Vancouver 124.2 (200 km) — Kamloops 143.8 (231.5 km)
**Alexandra Lodge:** For decades this Lodge and its predecessor were familiar stopping places. Nearly 150 years ago the Hudson's Bay Company's Brigade Trail passed here, with traces still evident several hundred feet up the bank. The only cleft in the mountain wall over which it could pass is very apparent on the skyline. The trail then dropped into the Anderson River Gorge and continued over extremely rough country to the Interior Plateau.

Old-timers who, many years ago, explored the first portion of this trail report finding several old campsites, even before the top of the first summit was reached. The short distance between camps bears out the difficulties and perils reported by the early traders:

"It was our intention to have reached the height of land today, but from the jaded state of our animals and the general confusion among the rear brigades we were obliged to camp in the woods . . . . Here again was a sad account of the goods, many pieces left on the road and three parties obliged to halt, separated one from another, night having overtaken them before they could reach camp."

In fact, so fraught with danger and hardship was this trail that a member of a party committed suicide here rather than carry on over the mountains. This perilous means of access to the Interior was abandoned shortly afterwards for a better route up the Coquihalla River.

Vancouver 125.1 (201.5 km) — Kamloops 142.9 (230 km)
**Alexandra Tunnel:** For people who yearn for the "good old days" here is what a miner called Radcliffe Quine wrote on April 22, 1861, after slogging his way northward:

"I tell you it is a hard road to travel. You have to carry your own blankets and food for over three hundred miles and take to the soft side of the road for your lodgings and at daylight get up and shake the dust off your blankets and cook your own food for the day and take the road again. When you get in the mines you have to pay up to a dollar a pound for everything you eat as it has to be carried with mules and horses on their backs with a pack saddle."

Vancouver 127.3 (205 km) — Kamloops 140.7 (226.5 km)

**Coopers Corner Rest Area:** Picnic tables beside a mountain creek but no toilets.

Vancouver 128 (206 km) — Kamloops 140 (225.5 km)

**Hells Gate and Ferrabee Tunnels:** Perhaps nowhere along the Canyon are the extreme difficulties of road building better illustrated than by this section of the Highway. The solid rock left no alternative but to break through it with tunnels. The original road was located precariously close to the river and rounded this obstacle on wooden trestles.

Simon Fraser, the first white explorer to venture down the river and after whom it is named, made his epic journey through 500 miles (805 km) of the river from Fort George in 1808. Of this section he noted:

"The water which rolls down this extraordinary passage in tumultuous waves and with great velocity had a frightful appearance; however, it being absolutely impossible to carry the canoes by land, all hands without hesitation embarked upon the mercy of this awful tide. Once engaged the die was cast, and the great difficulty consisted in keeping the canoes clear of the precipice on one side, and the gulfs formed by the waves on the other, then skimming along as fast as lightning."

Fraser's twenty-three companions were the famed voyageurs, men who had spent a lifetime in canoes, yet in one four-day period in the canyon they travelled only 30 miles (48 km) — and they were heading downstream. Finally the waters became too formidable even for Fraser and his men, and they left the river and proceeded overland.

This proved as dangerous as the river. As Fraser wrote: "An Indian climbed to the summit, and by means of a long pole drew us up, one after another. This work took three hours. Then we continued our course up and down, among hills, and along steep declivities of mountains, where hanging rocks and projecting cliffs at the edge of the bank of the river made the passage so small as to render it difficult at times, even for one person to pass. In places we were obliged to hand our guns from one to another, and the greatest precaution was required to pass singly free of encumbrances . . . . We had to pass where no human being should venture."

Vancouver 129.5 (208.5 km) — Kamloops 138.5 (223 km)

**Hells Gate with Fishways and Aerial Tram:** It's a long way down and a disappointing trip to many visitors who decide to walk. During spring high water which often lasts until July 15, the fishways may be under water. Then, too, the water is usually so muddy that fish cannot be seen.

It takes approximately fifteen minutes to go down; thirty minutes to make the climb back. Sturdy shoes and strong heart are definite assets. Fortunately, there is the aerial tramway and, for obvious reasons, it is very popular.

The fish ladders and Hells Gate and, inset, the sternwheeler *Skuzzy*, the only vessel to successfully battle her way through Hells Gate. (See page 66.)

**The History of the Fishways:** The vast network of waterways which forms the Fraser River drainage system has been the spawning grounds for millions of salmon since the last ice age some 9,000 years ago. In fact the Fraser River and its tributaries are home to more spawning salmon than any other waterway in the world. Before a slide and debris from heavy railway construction obstructed the river channel in 1913-14, as many as five million salmon were estimated to spawn beyond this spot each year. Although the fish could pass at certain low and high-water stages, there was an approximate range in river elevation of 30 ft. (9 m) when their progress was blocked because of the immense rapids caused by the slide.

In principle, the fishways provide an alternative route through the fast water. In these large concrete flumes, water velocity is reduced to 1.5 ft.

(.45 m) per second, whereas the velocity through Hells Gate often reached 25 ft. (7.5 m) per second. Although the water appears to flow the fastest just below the fishways, the irregular river walls create back eddies which allow the salmon to reach the fishways.

The flumes on either side of the river are 45 ft. (13.5 m) deep and above water during late summer and winter. They may be under water some 40-50 ft. (12-15 m) from May 15 to July 15 since the seasonal rise and fall of water reaches spectacular proportions. The river, under the foot bridge is 100 ft. (30 m) deep at low water but it can rise over 100 ft. (30 m), as was demonstrated in 1948. Since the fishways are under water for considerable periods of time, they are covered to keep out water-borne debris.

The mode of operation is quite different from the conventional fish ladders made up of short sections of flume rising in staircase fashion. Here, the entire flume is on an incline but is divided into sections by baffles.

The length of the right bank fishway (across the river) is 220 ft.

(66 m) and that of the left bank, 460 ft. (138 m). The former climbs 8 ft. (2.4 m) in elevation and the latter 6 ft. (2 m). Their width is 20 ft. (4 m), except for an upstream portion of the left bank fishway which is 12 ft. (3.6 m) wide. A tunnel 12 ft. (3.6 m) wide and 52 ft. (15.6 m) deep was built below the right bank fishway to pierce a rocky spur projecting into the river. This secondary river channel creates a large eddy just below the fishways which provides the struggling salmon with a place to rest. The complexities of the current are such that, although the top portion of the water speeds through the tunnel, the lower part actually runs back up the tunnel, giving a boost to fish taking this particular route. Although the river appears throttled between its confining walls, it is actually 110 ft. (33 m) across at the narrowest place.

**Hells Gate Airtram:** The enclosed airtram transports visitors to the west bank, providing a helicopter view of the awesome gorge on the 500-ft. (150-m) descent. At the bottom terminal are a gift shop specializing in Canadiana, dining room, picnic area and a comprehensive model of the fishways with a film and exhibit illustrating the salmon's four-year life cycle.

Behind the gift shop at the top terminal is a Stop of Interest — FRASER CANYON: "This awesome gorge has always been an obstacle to transportation. Indians used ladders and road builders hung 'shelves' to skirt its cliffs. Canoes rarely dared its whirlpools; only one sternwheeler fought it successfully. Railroads and highways challenged it with tunnels and bridges, but today man and nature still battle for supremacy."

**The sternwheeler** mentioned on the plaque was the *Skuzzy*, built by railway contractor Andrew Onderdonk (See Mile 105.9). During CPR construction in 1882-85 Onderdonk's main problem was getting material to his construction camps. The tolls on the Cariboo Road were costing him $10 per ton of freight. In addition to that levy, it was often necessary to ferry goods across the river in Indian canoes and in two ferry-boats he built, one at Chapman's Bar and one at Nicaragua Bluff. This method was not only slow but dangerous, especially at Nicaragua Bluff where a huge whirlpool was almost as wide as the river.

A ferryman named W. H. Holmes wrote an account of his experiences. Of the ferry at Chapman's Bar he noted: "A Swede was employed to run it. He, however, only made one trip. He swamped the boat and lost his freight; and at that moment a blast went off, and killed one of his crew. As soon as he landed, he started to run towards Yale, and he is supposed to be running yet."

To help solve his supply problem, Onderdonk decided to construct a sternwheel steamer. She was built at Spuzzum in the winter of 1881-82 and launched by Mrs. Onderdonk in the spring. Christened the *Skuzzy*, she was 120 ft. (36 m) long by 24 ft. (7.2 m) wide, her hull divided into twenty watertight compartments. It was later proved, in an accidental fashion, that she would still float with half her bottom ripped out.

The ship built, she now only required a captain and a crew. Usually one look at the boat and the Canyon sufficed to send prospective captains back to parts where the water didn't stand so much on edge.

Finally, drastic measures had to be taken, so word was sent to Captains S. R. and D. S. Smith. The daring steamboating feats of these two brothers on the Columbia River were legendary. They had run a steamer 1,000 miles (1,610 km) down the turbulent Snake River and another over the falls of the Willamette at Oregon City.

They obtained a crew of seventeen men and with a skilful engineer, started the ascent. At the end of seven days with the steam safety valve screwed shut they had managed to reach Hells Gate. One of those involved in the historic voyage was ferryboatman W. Holmes. He wrote:

"There was some very swift water at many of the bars, especially at China Bar, and there and further up I was called upon to use my ferry-boat, running out lines at different points. At this particular bar I ran out the line and got it tightened up, but with the steamer's power and the steam-winch we could only just get so far. The boat just hung there. Word was sent to the camps that were handy and over a hundred Chinese responded. Lines were run out and when they started to pull the boat just leaped over the rapid. Our next trouble was Hell's Gate which was the most dangerous place of all. In order to run out the lines I had to take my small boat up first and I had quite a risky time getting her through. When all was ready and the *Scuzzy* started up, the rush of water was so great that she was first dashed against one side of the wall of the canyon and tossed over against the other . . . the water rose and fell in awful cascades, and the poor *Scuzzy* rose and plunged like a ship in a heavy sea.

"The *Scuzzy* before she started up through the narrow and treacherous walls was a nice looking boat, but, when she had ascended through the gate, there was nothing of her left but the bare hull — the railings and guards on both sides had been ripped off, and she was scratched all over."

The *Skuzzy* performed notable service in supplying the upper construction camps. On completion of this section of railway she was dismantled and her engines put in a new *Scuzzy* on Kamloops Lake. Launched in 1885, she was 140 ft. (42 m) long and constructed in a record forty-four days.

There will never again be a boat of comparative size to make the trip through the Canyon. The impossible was done once and once only, although today river rafters plunge downstream through Hells Gate. The sport is not without hazard, however, and when one raft capsized only good luck saved some of those on board from drowning.

Vancouver 130.9 (210.8 km) — Kamloops 137.1 (220.7 km)

**Stop of Interest** — FRASER'S RIVER: " 'We could scarcely make our way even with our guns. We had to pass where no human being should venture; yet in those places there is a regular footpath . . . indented upon the very rocks.'

"So wrote Simon Fraser, explorer and fur-trader, in 1808, the first white man to descend the river which bears his name."

As travellers speed along the modern Highway, its tunnels, steep grades, massive fills and curves around rock faces provide an idea of the difficulties of building the Highway and of the incredible challenge confronting the miners until completion of the Wagon Road in 1863. One gold seeker, W. Champness, wrote:

"Some portions of our route lay across mountain ranges from whose summits we enjoyed most magnificent views, and down whose steep pine-forested sides we had to lead our horses singly, and with utmost care.

"In other parts of the journey, especially in the river gorges, our track conducted us along the most frightful precipices. There was no help for this, as we could select no route more passable. The river flows ofttimes through dark and awful gorges whose rocky sides tower perpendicularly from a thousand to fifteen hundred feet. By a series of zig-zag paths, often but a yard in width, man and beast have to traverse these scenes of grandeur. Sad and fatal accidents often occur, and horses and their owners are dashed to pieces on the rocks below, or drowned in the deep foaming waters rushing down the narrow defiles from the vast regions of mountain snow melting in the summer heat."

Vancouver 131.1 (211.1 km) — Kamloops 136.9 (220.4 km)

**China Bar Tunnel:** At 2,000 ft. (600 m) this is the longest of the seven tunnels and the last encountered by eastbound travellers. The one-mile (1.6 km) section of highway which includes the tunnel cost $5 million, the most expensive section of two-lane highway ever constructed in B.C. at that time. The tunnel replaced a section of the 1926 highway that terrified many travellers — especially during winter's ice and snow — since it clung to the cliffs with a sheer drop of several hundred feet (meters) into the rapids.

**War in the Canyon:** During the summer of 1858 amid the rocks of the Fraser

Hells Gate in 1868 with salmon drying on the racks. Salmon from the Fraser River and its tributaries provided much of the winter food for Interior B.C. Indians.
Opposite page: Hells Gate Airtram is a popular tourist attraction.

Canyon, whites and Indians engaged in a vicious war. Although the number killed is unknown, the dead exceeded by several times those killed on both sides in the subsequent 1885 Riel Rebellion. In June the bodies of twenty-nine mutilated miners were taken from the Fraser River at Fort Yale and another thirty-two downstream at Fort Hope. As already related in the text at Fort Yale, Edward Stout and his twenty-four companions were ambushed at what is today Jackass Mountain. They fought their way back to China Bar, only seven now alive. Two more were killed as they tried to build a protective rock barrier, the five survivors so badly wounded they could go no further. Then they heard gunfire below them — miners were coming to their rescue.

There were several causes for the uprising. Indians resented the whites invading their land and taking what they considered was their gold. Liquor was a factor, and the Indians claimed that the whites had violated their homes. Whatever the reasons, in June the Indians started murdering the miners, cutting off their heads and tossing them into the rapids of the river.

On July 27 the correspondent for the *Victoria Gazette* wrote:

"Dr. Spearm says the Indians at New York Bar were all drunk, and had driven the few whites on the Bar into one tent, where the latter were determined to make a stand, and if worse came to the worst, for all to die fighting like men. The Indians were armed with guns and knifes. There were two dead bodies found in the river, presumed to have been murdered by the red devils, yesterday."

By August, Yale was crowded with miners who fled the Canyon, the fate of those who stayed revealed in the headless bodies that floated downstream. Under Charles Rouse, some forty men formed an armed company and headed into the Canyon. At Boston Bar they met more miners who had banded together for self-defence and here fought the first major

battle with the Indians. Henry M. Snider, a correspondent for the *San Francisco Bulletin*, later reported:

"On the 14th a fight with the Indians took place, which lasted three hours, and resulted in the complete rout of the savages. Seven of the Indians are known to have been killed, and a number wounded. One white man only was wounded, and that slightly in the arm. About 150 white men were in the fight."

As related in Heritage House book, *Tales of Conflict: Indian-White Murders and Massacres in Pioneer British Columbia:*

"Snyder also told of another fight. James Stewart, on arriving at Fort Yale, reported that he and a party of miners had been attacked at the head of the Big Canyon. He said that nine Indians, including a chief, had been slain, a number wounded and captured. The miners had found Mexican sashes on the bodies of the dead Indians. These, Stewart declared, had been taken from Cornish, Scottish and American miners. The incensed whites fired five Indian villages, burning their stocks of food.

"The miners determined to put an end to the trouble. Word to the effect that a strong column was to be sent against the savages brought men hurrying to Fort Yale. Four companies were organized. Snyder, the news correspondent, had command of fifty-one composing the 'Pike Guards.' Later he was reinforced by thirty-one late arrivals. The 'French Company,' under John Centras, numbered eighty-two. There were two smaller companies, numbering about twenty men each, under leadership of a man named Graham and another called Galloway. Captain Graham's outfit was known as the 'Whatcom Guards.' These smaller organized bands were opposed to the policy of Snyder and Centras, which aimed at conciliation. They favored extermination of the Indians.

"The Pike Guards and French Company led the way, offering peace to the natives. It was readily accepted. Graham, who followed, however, made it apparent that he did not respect the white flags that Snyder had given to the Indians who expressed a willingness to submit to the white men's authority. That night Graham's camp was attacked by Indians who killed Graham and his chief lieutenant, James Shaw.

"Snyder's mission of conciliation and peace, and Graham's unhappy fate, virtually ended the organized fighting."

Vancouver 134.3 (216.3 km) — Kamloops 133.7 (215.2 km)

**Anderson River and Bridge**, named after A. C. Anderson, a young clerk in the fur trade and in charge of Fort Alexandria (between Williams Lake and Quesnel). Impatient with the negotiations over international boundaries and trade routes, he volunteered to explore ways of reaching the coast from the interior. In 1847 he located the dangerous Brigade Trail, via the Nicola, Coldwater and Anderson Rivers. He eventually reached the Fraser River at a point opposite Spuzzum.

**The Thompson Indians:** Interior Salish is another name for the Indians living along the Fraser River from Spuzzum to Lillooet, along the Thompson River northward to Ashcroft, and along the Nicola River eastward to Nicola Lake.

The Thompson Indian Territory was divided into two main parts — the area below Lytton and that above. The Lower Thompson Indians,

Spuzzum, population 91, calls itself "The Smallest and Friendliest Town in the West."

thanks for Visiting Spuzzm.. come again

At Boston Bar access to the west side of the Fraser River is over a section of the 1863 Cariboo Wagon Road.

The CNR station at Boston Bar was built in 1915 as part of the then Canadian Northern Railway. In B.C. it is one of only two original stations still in operation.

BOSTON BAR  MONTREAL 4436 KM
VANCOUVER 202 KM

numbering over 2,000 in 1858, lived along the river from near Siska south to Spuzzum. Generation after generation of individual families wintered on the same small river terrace. In 1896 there were nineteen villages between Siska and Spuzzum, although the population had been greatly depleted by smallpox.

This dread disease was brought into the country in 1863. The Indians, packed in their keekwilee houses, were stricken unmercifully by this epidemic, from which there was no escape. Some fled to the mountains, only to collapse and die by the trail. Others sought to cure themselves in the sweat houses, but to no avail. Almost one third of the population died.

The Lower Thompson Indians depended largely on fish for food but were heavy meat-eaters when game could be obtained. They experienced certain climatic conditions similar to those of the Coast regions, and therefore copied some living habits from the Coast Indians. Cedar bark was used for mats and cedar roots for basket making. As deer were scarce, robes woven of mountain goat wool were worn. During summer and wet weather the tribe went barefoot. The rich wore moccasins during the winter and, although it sounds extremely "fishy," the poor people made floppy shoes of dog-salmon skins.

**Hazel shrubs** which grow in this area were important to the Indians since from them they made a stout rope. They grow with slender straight stems to form a loose bush about 10 ft. (3 m) high. During August and September the hazel nut is wrapped in a greenish, stocking-like husk. In the winter months, slim yellow catkins ornament the graceful branches.

Vancouver 136.3 (219.5 km) — Kamloops 131.7 (212 km)
**Boston Bar:** A small community with tourist services that include service stations, accommodation, stores and restaurants. In 1858 Boston Bar was only a name among others like Dutchman's Bar, China Bar, Island Bar, and Fargo Bar. With the building of the Cariboo Wagon Road and later, the CPR, a small village began to form. The present town occupies a length of benchland immediately above the Fraser River.

**Fraser River and Bridge:** This bridge at the north end of Boston Bar gives access to the community of North Bend and gravel side roads. From 1939 to 1986 vehicle access to North Bend was by a unique aerial ferry with a one-car capacity. It spanned 960 ft. (288 m) between loading points and swayed 120 ft. (36 m) over the Fraser River during low water, with local boosters claiming it was the only one of its kind in the world. While less adventurous, the modern bridge is much more convenient.

From North Bend a secondary road heads along the west bank of the Fraser some 30 miles (48 km) to just above the junction of the Fraser-Thompson Rivers. There a ferry crosses the Thompson above Lytton. (See "Side Roads and Back Roads" at Mile 87.9)

Vancouver 142 (228.7 km) — Kamloops 126 (202.8 km)
**Ainslee Creek and Bridge:** Before the Highway was reconstructed the road swung far up the creek in search of a low crossing place. For this reason the bridge is 475 ft. (145 m) above the creek, one of the highest of its kind in Canada, and cuts 3 miles (5 km) off the old route.

Vancouver 143.8 (231.5 km) — Kamloops 124.2 (200 km)

**Boothroyd, or Jamieson's Flat:** Now part of an Indian reserve with modern homes, this flat was the site of a pioneer roadhouse and welcome respite to the mule- and ox-team freighters after the difficult haul out of Nine-Mile Creek.

**Early Express and Stagecoach Days:** Pictorial records of the Cariboo Wagon Road depict almost continuous caravans of mules, oxen, and horses pulling everything from a light cart to heavy freight wagons and stagecoaches. Much of this traffic was operated by one company.

In 1858, Billy Ballou started the rudiments of an express service but, several years after, had a competitor in F. J. Barnard, probably the most energetic postman in the world. He started his career in 1860 by carrying a pack between Yale and the Cariboo goldfields. This 380-mile (610-km) jaunt, each way, was done on foot. No wonder he charged $2 for letter delivery and sold papers at $1 apiece. Having eliminated his competitor in 1862, Barnard organized Barnard's Express and at 5 a.m. on May 12, 1864, left Yale on the first stagecoach trip up the new Cariboo Road. Charles G. Major was driver on the historic trip and among the nine passengers were Robert Stevenson and H. M. Steele, two of the most successful miners of the gold rush. On the return trip, Stephen Tingley was the driver. He was to continue driving for more than thirty years, eventually buying the firm.

Barnard took exceptional pride in the quality of his horses and equipment. Coaches of fourteen-passenger capacity were drawn by from four to six spirited horses. To keep up his exacting schedule, the horses were changed every 13-17 miles (20-27 km). Such frequent changes necessitated keeping 250 horses on hand, of which 150 were continually in harness.

When the Cariboo goldfields were at their peak of productivity, it was Barnard's Express that brought the yellow wealth to the coast. His express coaches frequently carried up to $150,000 in gold and, in 1865, safely conveyed over $3 million in gold dust and nuggets.

Barnard was aware of the danger of robberies. An early paper reported: "Mr. Barnard has fitted an iron burglar-proof safe into each of his wagons. He has the chests constructed with detonating powder in the interstices between the plates, and on any attempt being made to open them with a chisel they would inevitably explode with the force of a bomb-shell. The safes are also fitted with combination locks, known only to the principals at each terminus . . . ."

Vancouver 146.7 (236.2 km) — Kamloops 121.3 (195.3 km)

**Indian Cemetery:** Although there are many Indian burial places in the Canyon, only a few are visible from the Highway. In the past each group of families had its own burial ground. This was carefully chosen, in a conspicuous place, some distance from the village. Until 1890, it was the regular practice for wealthy Indians to open the graves of relatives a year or two after death and at intervals thereafter. The bones were carefully gathered up each time, wiped, and put in a new blanket. Often, personal property such as weapons and ornaments was buried with the body.

**Coast meets Interior:** While it is impossible to define a precise boundary

Indians have lived in the Fraser Canyon for some 9,000 years. Opposite is a Chief and, above, a Chief's grave in 1868. After the Missionaries arrived the Indians adopted the white method of burial, resulting in graveyards such as the one below along the Highway between Boston Bar and Lytton.

between the two regions, plants and trees are now changing very noticeably. The shaggy, dark green cedar, characteristic of a wetter climate, gives way to the airy yellow pine of the dry Interior. The large Douglas fir of the moist coastal slopes also changes here to the shorter, more scrubby fir of the Interior.

**A common plant** bordering the Highway in both coast and interior climates is the mullein. It is easily identified by its large olive-green leaves from which protrudes a spike up to 5 ft. (1.5 m) high, studded with small yellow flowers. In winter and early spring only a brownish, cane-like stalk remains.

Vancouver 149.3 (240.4 km) — Kamloops 118.7 (191.1 km)
**Tilton Creek:** This creek commemorates F. G. Tilton, superintendent and chief engineer for CPR contractor Andrew Onderdonk. It also illustrates why rebuilding the Highway was so expensive since it sits on an earth fill about 170 ft. (51 m) deep.

Vancouver 150.4 (242.2 km) — Kamloops 117.6 (189.3 km)
**Start of the ascent up Jackass Mountain:** The modern highway has a much better grade than the original because engineers started their cut some 600 ft. (180 m), or sixty storeys, above the level of the old road.

**Old Jackass Mountain Mission:** Long a landmark, the Mission was at the bottom of the mountain in a small orchard. In bygone days, the Cariboo Wagon Road wound through the orchard and passed almost in front of the frame building that served the large pioneer district.

Archdeacon Small was the preacher and no man in the wild rugged country was more admired and respected. When it became known that he was being replaced there was considerable speculation about whether the newcomer would fit into the rough atmosphere. Fears were allayed when he prefaced his first sermon by saying that his introduction to the Mission had been an exciting one. He had witnessed no less a personage than Archdeacon Small dashing among the apple trees, butcher knife in hand, pursuing the raw material (a sheep) for the welcoming dinner.

**Thompson's Patent Road Steamers:** Six massive road steamers and six stalwart engineers arrived from England in 1871 to brave the wilderness road and usher in a new era of transportation. In spring the first of the vehicles left Yale. Pulling 6 tons (tonnes) it reached Spuzzum the first day, Boston Bar the second, and Jackass Mountain the third. Here the journey to Cariboo ended. Thompson, when he designed his gear system, had not counted on such grades as Jackass Mountain, and the road steamers could do little more than steam. After the failure of this "modern" venture it was back to horse-, mule- and ox-drawn freight wagons which continued to serve the Cariboo for almost another fifty years.

Vancouver 152.2 (245 km) — Kamloops 115.8 (186.5 km)
**Summit of Jackass Mountain and Stop of Interest** — JACKASS MOUNTAIN: "A memorial to a mule. Wearied by its struggle over the steep, twisting Cariboo Road, one loaded mule reared, bucked, and fell to its death in the canyon. The long stream of freight animals closed their ranks and plodded onward to the distant Cariboo goldfields."

This section of Highway, high above the river, is one of the more spectacular stretches, notched into solid rock with the river a shining ribbon far below. The terraces across the river show the height of the old river bed many thousands of years ago. On this side, the glacial fill has been completely washed away, leaving the very ancient canyon walls.

**Canoe trip, anyone?** While gazing far down into the depths of the canyon with its tumbling and swirling waters, do you wonder what it would be like to travel in a frail canoe? A vivid description was penned by Simon Fraser on his epic voyage of exploration in 1808:

"Here the channel contracts to about 40 yards, and is enclosed by two precipices of immense height which, bending towards each other, make it narrow above and below. The water which rolls down this extraordinary passage in tumultuous waves and with great velocity had a frightful appearance. However, it being absolutely impossible to carry the canoes by land, all hands without hesitation embarked, as it were, a *corps perdu* (a lost legion) upon the mercy of this awful tide. Once engaged, the die was cast. Our great difficulty consisted in keeping the canoes within the medium or *fil d'eau*; that is, clear of the precipice on the one side and from the gulfs formed by the waves on the other. Thus, skimming along as fast as lightning, the crews, cool and determined, followed each other in awful silence, and when we arrived at the end we stood gazing at each other in silent congratulation at our narrow escape from total destruction."

HORSE, MULE AND OX TRANSPORT: All three played their distinctive part in maintaining the flow of passengers, freight and supplies over the pioneer road — and even camels were tried!

**Horses** were generally used for stage and express coach service with two or three teams providing the horse power. The heavy freight wagons often required six or eight teams and, drawn by the long line of straining horses, made an impressive sight. As with the mule teams, the driver sometimes rode the first animal on the left side and controlled them all by jerking one line. Such a system gave rise to the driver being known as a "jerk-line driver."

**Mules** were considered the most suitable animals for carrying individual loads. The caravans of from sixteen to sixty pack-animals, each carrying upwards of 250 lbs. (113 kg), no longer appeared after 1866. After that, the mules were used most frequently on the freight service. Sometimes as many as twenty-four would be hitched to one or more wagons.

**Bull Teams** were made up of patient, plodding oxen. Twelve to sixteen yoke, or pairs, of these animals drawing one load was the common practice when a full day's journey equalled the number of miles (kilometers) a car now travels in a few minutes.

**Camels:** Of all the means of transport to the Cariboo, camels seem the most unlikely. Yet they were used, although not for long. In the book, *Wagon Road North: Historic Photos from 1863 of the Cariboo Gold Rush*, is the following account of the venture:

"It all started in 1862 when John C. Calbreath of Lillooet purchased

23 camels in San Francisco for $300 each. Calbreath, however, was apparently only an agent for a syndicate that included Frank Laumeister, Adam Heffley, and Henry Ingram. In this he was fortunate.

"In theory the project seemed sound. A camel could carry about 800 pounds compared to a mule's 300, could travel 30 to 40 miles a day to a mule's 15, and could go for days without food and water whereas a mule required both quite frequently. As a bonus camels thrive in hot country and in summer, sections of the Cariboo are hot and dry.

"In May, 1862, the camels arrived at Port Douglas on a barge towed by the sternwheeler *Flying Dutchman*. Laumeister was apparently in charge since he was most frequently mentioned in the uproar which followed. The syndicate hoped to earn $60,000 the first season, but the camels soon proved the difference between hope and reality. They probably had good points, but these were effectively counterbalanced. One of their bad habits was attacking anything they didn't like — and they quickly showed their dislikes to be many.

"As one beast came down the sternwheeler's gangway it saw a prospector's mule and quickly bit and kicked it into oblivion. The camels, though, soon displayed a good point, possibly their only one. They were completely impartial, biting and kicking anything and everything from mules to oxen, from horses to men. Complementing their mean temperament was their odor — so potent that it alone caused pack animals to bolt. Even washing the camels in scented water didn't help. The "Dromedary Express," as it became known, soon was hated throughout the Cariboo.

"Another shortcoming of the camels proved to be their hoofs. They were built for sand and were no match for the rocks and hardpan of the Fraser and Cariboo. Laumeister tried fitting them with shoes made of canvas and rawhide but this was only part of his problems. The other packers now unanimously disliked camels. Besides threatening to sue for damages, they started a petition requesting that camels be banned.

"In 1864, Laumeister disbanded his brigade, probably because the animals's hoofs couldn't stand the rocky terrain. The camels gradually vanished into history. According to historian Bruce Ramsey, some died in winter storms, others were shot for meat, a few were kept as curiosity items. The last died near Grande Prairie in the northern Okanagan in 1905."

Vancouver 154.1 (248.2 km) — Kamloops 113.9 (183.3 km)

**Kanaka Bar**, a gold-rush river bar named after the Hawaiians who took part in the gold rush. As the miners fought their way upstream in 1858-59 they found gold along the shore and on virtually all of the bars. One miner wrote:

"We found gold everywhere, and my only surprise was that a region so auriferous should have remained so long unproclaimed and hidden from the gaze of civilization. I found a very choice quartz specimen, six ounces in weight, which contained at least four ounces of gold, half jutting out of the sand on the river's bank. During this day's work seven nuggets, varying from about half an ounce to five ounces in weight were picked up, while the average yield of dust was no less than four ounces each man, and all I had to work with was a gold pan."

# STEAM TO CARIBOO!

## *The British Columbia*
## GENERAL TRANSPORTATION COMPANY

Will place Four of THOMSON'S PATENT ROAD STEAM-
ERS on the route between **Yale** and **Barkerville** in the First
Week in April, and will be prepared to enter into Contracts for
the conveyance of Freight from **Yale** to **Soda Creek** in Eight
Days. Through Contracts will be made as soon as the condition
of the road above Quesnelmouth permits.

Rates of Passage will be advertised in due time.

**Above:** Stagecoaches and freight wagons at Boothroyd stopping place in 1868.

**Top left:** An 1868 photo of freight teams slowly wending up Jackass Mountain, steepest grade in the Fraser River Canyon.

**Opposite:** Despite the optimistic 1871 advertisement, road steamers were a complete failure, as were the camels. At right is one of the camels used for packing supplies to the Cariboo in 1862. It died in the Okanagan in 1905.

**A Million Dollar Dredge:** Shipped from England, this bulky piece of machinery was installed near Kanaka Bar in 1906. Like similar ventures, it was doomed to failure. Before operations could even get under way, it iced-over during a winter storm and sank. In 1959 an attempt was made to salvage the machinery, but it turned into tragedy when the diver died underwater from an unknown cause.

**Kanaka Bar Derailment:** Although the final spike wasn't driven on the CPR until 1885, as sections of line were completed they were immediately put into service. One was between New Westminster through the Canyon to the new community of Ashcroft on the Thompson River.

As passenger and freight traffic increased derailments became common, a not unexpected development since the Canyon section had been built under government contract. When Cornelius Van Horne, the dynamic general manager of the CPR, saw the Canyon trackage he commented that there were "too bloody many trestles" and the line was "the worst he'd ever seen."

One derailment in 1884 was at Kanaka Bar when the mail train ran over a horse. Although the engine and freight cars plunged 100 ft. (30 m) down an embankment, the passenger car with its sleeping occupants stayed on the tracks.

Early railroading was a nightmare with trains colliding in dark tunnels, backing into each other round sharp curves, jumping the rails to teeter on the brink of precipices, and even plunging through trestles. Most of the confusion was caused because there was no way to turn engines around at the eastern end of the tracks. Engineers went forward one way, then backed up for the return trip. Believing that he who runs away today lives to work another day, train crewmen became adept at leaping in the nick of time.

Other trainmen were not so fortunate. One fireman lost his life when a bridge 10 miles (16 km) east of Spences Bridge collapsed in the darkness. At Yale a locomotive and all cars except the passenger car plunged through a trestle. Two crew members were killed instantly. Scarcely two weeks later, another engine plunged from the roadbed, killing two and injuring two more.

Vancouver 157.5 (253.6 km) — Kamloops 110.5 (177.9 km)
**Siska Creek and Bridge:** Siska is the Indian word for "unpredictable" and refers to the water flow in the creek. Here twin railway bridges cross the Fraser River. The reason is that the CPR which was built before the Canadian Northern (now Canadian National) swung its line from the east to the west bank, forcing the CNR to switch from the west to the east bank since nowhere in the Canyon was it possible to place both lines on the same side of the river for any appreciable distance.

Vancouver 159.9 (257.5 km) — Kamloops 108.1 (174 km)
**Scuppa Rest Area** with picnic tables and rural toilets. The peaks across the river are part of the Cantilever Range of the Coast Mountains. Skihist Mountain, the tallest, soars to 9,495 ft. (2,944 m) and is home to grizzly and black bears, mountain goat and other wildlife.

Vancouver 162.9 (262.3 km) — Kamloops 105.1 (169.2 km)
**Junction of Highways 1-12:** Although today's highway bypasses Lytton, the original road loops through the community and rejoins the Trans-Canada about 1 mile (1.6 km) ahead.

**Lytton** was the historic site of an Indian village appropriately called Cumchin, or "Great Forks." As elsewhere in the Canyon, fish was the natives' main food supply and they caught huge quantities. In the 1840s HBC Chief Trader John Tod mentioned that in just one expedition to Lytton he got 50,000 dried salmon.

The first whites to see the area were Simon Fraser and his voyageurs. They arrived on June 19, 1808, and camped overnight. Fraser named the river after his friend and fellow explorer David Thompson, whom he thought was exploring its headwaters. Thompson, however, never saw the river that bears his name. The river he was exploring was the Columbia, which he followed to its mouth.

Lytton was first known to the miners as "The Forks," but the name was later changed to Lytton after Sir Edward Bulwer Lytton, Secretary of State for the Colonies. On May 14, 1859, the following description appeared in the *Victoria Gazette:*

"The 'City' of Lytton is beautifully situated on a high plat of green sward, as level and smooth as a carpeted floor . . . . The town numbers twenty-six houses, built mostly of logs, one or two being very nicely finished . . . . Just above the level on which the town is located, Thompson river empties its clear cold flood into the murky Fraser, presenting a singular contrast as the two streams flow side by side along the front of the town."

**Highway 12 to Lillooet** begins near the center of downtown Lytton. It is 43 miles (69 km) to Lillooet over a paved road which follows the east bank of the Fraser River.

**Lillooet,** population 2,400, is now a quiet community, different from the days when it was the original Mile Zero on the Cariboo Wagon Road, and in the early 1860s the second largest community north of San Francisco. It supported thirteen saloons, among other liquor outlets. In all, twenty-five places were licensed to sell liquor.

A Stop of Interest sign which overlooks the community summarizes its lusty days: LILLOOET: "Here was the gateway to gold! Yellow gold-lined bars of the Fraser and beyond was the lure of the Cariboo. Like a magnet it drew thousands of miners on the long Harrison Trail through the Coast Mountains. From this focal point the first Cariboo Wagon Road was started northward in 1858. The trail-end at Lillooet became Mile 0 on the new road to riches."

Late in 1858 a trail had been slashed around the Fraser Canyon to Lillooet and in 1860 it was widened to a wagon road. From Port Douglas on Harrison Lake the road led overland 38 miles (60.8 km) to Lillooet Lake. Here a steamer, *Lady of the Lake,* connected to a 30-mile- (48-km-) long road which led from Lillooet to Anderson Lake. Service on 19-mile- (30-km-) long Anderson Lake was provided by another sternwheeler, the *Marzelle.* From Anderson Lake 1.5 miles (2.4 km) of road led to 23-mile- (36.8-km-) long Seton Lake and another steamer, the *Champion.* From Seton Lake

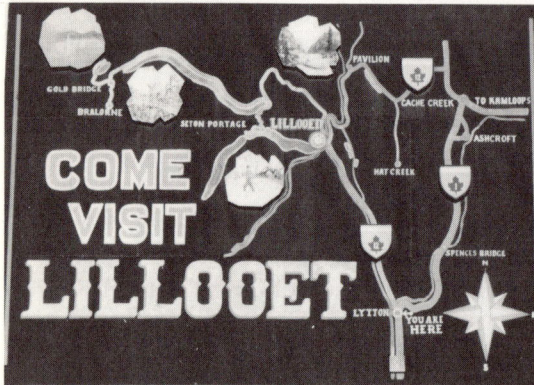

Lytton in the 1890s, with the Thompson River flowing in from the left.

From Lytton paved Highway 12 gives access to Lillooet, an 1860s gold-rush community.

Below: The Trans-Canada bypasses Lytton as it leaves the Fraser River and heads up the Thompson.

it was 3 miles (4.8 km) by road to Lillooet. Then in 1861 Gustavus Blin Wright began work on 47 miles (75.6 km) of road from Lillooet to a point that became known as Clinton.

But this route was not satisfactory. Wright's road climbed over a 4,000 ft. (1,200 m) mountain and grades were steep and hazardous. From Port Douglas to Lillooet freight had to be transferred from steamer to wagon and wagon to steamer at least eight times, each transfer causing considerable inconvenience for travellers and an increase in freight rates. For this reason Governor Douglas decided to embark on his bold venture of building a wagon road up the Fraser and Thompson Canyons. Completion of the road in 1863 bypassed Lillooet and its glory days ended. Today its main links to the gold-rush era are St. Mary's Church, built in 1861 and still in use; a main street wide enough for an oxen-drawn freight wagon to make a U-turn; and a highway bridge over the Fraser called "Bridge of the 23 Camels."

From Lillooet an alternate route to Vancouver is via the Duffey Lake Road to Pemberton, Whistler Ski Resort and Howe Sound over a route which is mostly paved; another alternate route is back to Highway 97 just north of Cache Creek via Marble Canyon over paved Highway 12; or to Clinton on Highway 97 over Pavilion Mountain. The latter route is gravel and dirt, little changed from the original built in 1861.

(For the benefit of southbound travellers, we will again mention that there is a series of maps and guide books available on this region and the hundreds of miles (kilometers) of other side roads west of the Fraser and Thompson Rivers. See Mile 87.9 in the text.)

**Dredging for Gold:** Van Winkle Bar is the extensive gravel flat across the river and slightly upstream from Lytton. The possibility of wealth in its hidden gravels launched still another mining venture. An English company built a steel dredge which was shipped to Lytton and assembled there. When finished it presented an imposing sight, for it was no less than 100 ft. (30 m) long and 30 ft. (9 m) wide. The business end was a long ladder-like boom providing support for a revolving belt on which thirty-two buckets were fixed. But Van Winkle Bar was definitely not the place where dreams come true, so the outfit moved to Kanaka Bar. Here, the heavy structure lay idle and then sank, another of the many dredges that failed. In fact, none so far have proved successful. Why do dredges fail? One veteran workman summarized the problem: "The river gives you only one chance. Make one mistake, or have something go wrong, and the river wins."

**Where Did the Gold Come From?:** In its molten state gold was squeezed into cracks in the rocks which formed the mountains. As the rocks were ground away by glaciers or eroded over hundreds of thousands of years, the gold was released. Then it was scattered throughout the enormous gravel deposits left by the glaciers. As water cut one channel after another through this gravel, the gold, being a heavy metal, sank to the bottom and was concentrated in each successively lower bed. These conditions, carried out repeatedly during tens of thousands of years, led to the exceedingly rich bars that were scattered along such a great length of the present river. This type of gold is known as "placer" gold.

Mountain goat are among wildlife which inhabit the mountains flanking the Fraser and Thompson Canyons. In addition, the area shown near Lytton on the opposite photo is home to a herd of elk introduced some years ago.

Although the bulk of gold was taken from the lower bars, most of the high terraces still contain some of the yellow flakes. The early miners found that the valuable gravels consisted of a yellowish layer less than a foot (30 cm) thick, lying not far below the surface of the gravel. This yellowish layer, usually associated with a bouldery wash, evidently marked the bed of the old stream which was later covered with a shallow accumulation of debris and soil. Because of water shortages, most of these terraces have never been worked, so the gold is still there. The big question is, of course, where?

But there is not only placer gold in this region. In the 1860s prospectors found gold in the gravel of Bridge River some 50 miles (80 km) up the Fraser River from Lytton. While there was nothing extraordinary in their find, some years later hardrock miners appeared and two mines resulted — Bralorne and Pioneer. They eventually closed, but not before yielding some 4 million ounces (11.5 million grams) worth then about $100 million — over $1 billion at today's price of gold.

**The Thompson River:** From Lytton the Trans-Canada Highway follows the Thompson River to Kamloops. For miles the Highway is only a few steps from the river. In fact, in some areas engineers had to build the Highway on cribbing right into the river channel.

The Thompson runs through dry belt country all the way to Kamloops.

Only a few inches (centimeters) of rain fall a year and summers can be hot, with Lytton recording the highest summer temperature in B.C. — a toasty 111°F (44°C). On the hillside Ponderosa pine parkland carpeted with bunchgrass is a complete change from the massive cedar, fir and dense undergrowth characteristic of the Fraser Canyon.

**Indian tobacco,** found in the hot, arid valleys north of Lytton, is a limby-looking plant about 18 inches (45 cm) high, very similar to the garden flower called nicotiana. The leaves are scattered and rather narrow, but it is the flower that forms the most distinctive feature. It is greenish-white, about 1 inch (2.5 cm) long, and shaped like a small tube, or trumpet. The prolonged blooming period extends from mid-May into September.

Indian tobacco was used by the Thompson River Indians from time immemorial since smoking played an important role in various ceremonial rites. The leaves were dried then blended with bear-berry leaves.

Vancouver 164.1 (264.3 km) — Kamloops 103.9 (167.2 km)
**Rocky Mountain elk** were released here in a co-operative program by the B.C. Fish and Wildlife Branch and the National and Historic Parks Branch. The elks' main range is east of the Highway and they can sometimes be seen with binoculars. This band is the reason for the highway signs in this area advising motorists to watch for elk.

Elk are the second largest member of the deer family, ranging in size between moose and mule deer. A mature bull may weigh up to 1,000 pounds (453 kg) and females up to 700 (317 kg). While grass and herbs make up probably 80 per cent of their diet, they also eat the shoots of young deciduous trees and, if pressed, even conifers. Although they once ranged over much of Central and Southern B.C., they are now reduced to a few pockets except in the East Kootenay where they are relatively abundant.

Vancouver 165.2 (265 km) — Kamloops 102.8 (165.5 km)

**Giant cleft, or Scarp:** Across the Thompson River is an unique rock formation that looks as if a sharp-crested mountain had been split lengthways and one half thrown away, leaving a tremendous cliff for one side. Some geologists theorize that it may have resulted from a fault, or sinking, of a portion of the earth's surface. Another possible explanation is that two different types of rock formation came in contact along this line. Because one was much softer than the other it gradually eroded, leaving a high vertical face of hard rock. This latter explanation gains strength from the fact that the rocks southward from the scarp are reddish-colored, hinting at their volcanic origin, while the cliff itself is of greyish-green granite with many irregular pink-colored bands.

**Forest Fires:** For decades following the 1860s gold rush, forest fires swept the countryside in devastating infernoes. Miners and early settlers were very casual about forest fires. It was "only burning trees, nothin' to worry about as long as it doesn't get into town." Indians once encouraged edible root plants to grow by burning sections of forest.

At lower left is a section of the original Cariboo Wagon Road in Skihist Provincial Park near Lytton. Over it from the early 1860s to the early 1880s rumbled stagecoaches and massive freight wagons drawn by oxen, mules or horses.

The magnitude of the fires is evident from the following news item in the September 29, 1868, *Cariboo Sentinel* at Barkerville:

"NO MAIL — We are this week without any mail or express from the lower country, owing, it is said, to the steamer's not being able to reach Yale until Thursday evening last, instead of the Sunday previous. The delay of the steamer was caused by smoke from the extensive fires which have been raging on the banks of the river between Yale and New Westminster."

Vancouver 168 (270.5 km) — Kamloops 100 (161 km)

**Skihist Provincial Park:** This popular park has 68 campsites set amidst Ponderosa pine, flush toilets, and picnic area across the Highway with a spectacular view of the Thompson River Canyon. In the park is a section of the 1863 Cariboo Wagon Road over which has travelled stagecoaches and freight wagons pulled by horses, oxen or mules; miners trudging back from the goldfields, some wealthy, the majority with only the clothes they wore; mule pack trains and even the camels. A plaque contains the following background information:

"CARIBOO WAGON ROAD: Ghosts of many miners may be travelling this old road. The Cariboo Road, stretching nearly 400 miles from Yale to Barkerville, was built to bring supplies and people to the booming goldfields of the interior.

" 'BS'ing' in 1863 meant 'bull slinging' — driving a team of oxen pulling two or three ten-ton freight wagons. Mining town streets were then set out 124 feet wide so that the bull teams could turn around. Camels were brought in because they could carry much more than a mule. They bit and kicked everything that moved, and smelled so badly that horses and mules would bolt their loads and sometimes fell off the road to their deaths.

"A fast BX stage carrying mail, passengers, express and gold covered

the distance from Barkerville to Ashcroft in four days. Way stations about every eighteen miles had fresh horses harnessed and waiting so that the fast trot could be maintained all the way."

At the picnic site is a Stop of Interest — THOMPSON CANYON: "Water cutting deeply into the pre-glacial floor of this valley over countless centuries, has gradually eroded the almost vertical dykes of the mountain of solid rock. The awesome display of crags and cliffs is vivid evidence of the might of the river and the ceaseless power of water at work. In places like this, man sees his true size."

The view down the Canyon shows the white-crested waters of the azure Thompson River running between massive walls carved from the solid rock. Colored cliffs rise above the railroad and, in the background, high peaks dominate the lower, more rounded mountains. The sharp crest to the right is Siwhe Mountain, 9,280 ft. (2,780 m) high, with the slightly lower mass of 9,010-ft. (2,700-m) Stein Mountain occupying the center horizon. To the extreme left is Skihist Mountain, elevation 8,660 ft. (2,600 m). All the names are of Indian origin.

Erosive action of wind and water has cut and grooved the mass of mountains across the river into myriad gullies and ravines. Under early morning or late afternoon lighting, when shadows sharpen the crags and spurs, this group of mountains present a picture of bold magnificence.

**Mountain goats** are part of the wildlife on 6,132 ft. (2,044 m) Mt. Lytton which rises behind Skihist Park and is part of the Cascade Mountains. Mountain goats are misnamed because they are not in fact true goats. Their closest relative is the chamois of the European Alps. Goats can be recognized by their long cream-colored coats and thin black horns on both male and female. They are grazing animals and very adaptable since they range from sea level to the rocks, crags and glaciers of mountains up to 7,500 ft. (2,258 m) and more.

Scientists believe that they arrived in North America over 100,000 years ago when a land bridge, which is now the Bering Sea, connected the continents. During the ice age they drifted southward ahead of the advancing ice sheets, then returned as the ice melted. There are an estimated 100,000 in B.C., more than in any other region of North America.

**Why the Arid Valleys?** Why are valleys north of Lytton parched and barren when they are only a few miles (kilometers) from the humid Coast Mountain area? This phenomenon occurs when warm, moist currents of air are swept up and up in their passage over the Coast Range barrier. Cooled by the low temperatures at such high elevations, they precipitate all their moisture. The air, thus dried, flows down the eastern slopes and grows warmer with decreasing elevation. In this warm dry condition, the air quickly absorbs moisture and consequently dries out the first valleys it encounters. In the spring these winds, called "chinooks," strip the snow from the ground in miraculous fashion.

**Yellow, or Ponderosa, pines** are the more prominent evergreen trees. They have an uncanny ability to grow just far enough apart to subsist on the meager rainfall allotted to each. The bark peels off, or exfoliates, in thin yellowish jig-saw puzzle shapes. It is usually extremely dry, burns with a good heat and little smoke. These features were valued by Indian war parties who used "the enemies' firewood" when on their expeditions of plunder, adventure or revenge. Another treasured quality of the yellow pine bark was that its ashes quickly cooled and it was difficult for enemy scouts to tell when the fire had been made.

**Spring Sunflowers, or Balsam Root:** No wild flower in British Columbia displays a more colorful or generous show than do the clusters of bright yellow flowers that cover the Interior river benches and mountain slopes. Blooming during April-May, they give a yellow sheen to far slopes which is particularly effective against the soft green background of spring grass.

The balsam root had many uses among the natives. The seeds, very rich and oily, were eaten raw or mixed with deer grease and boiled by means of hot stones. The roots were eaten raw, after being soaked in water overnight, or were roasted with much care and ceremony in large pits.

**Saskatoon Berry, or Service Berry,** grows from coast to coast but is predominant among the sparse growth of the Interior. It is a common shrub along this section and grows from 6-12 feet (1.8-3.6 m) high. The leaves are little more than 1 inch (2.5 cm) long and the branches all point upward, providing a spreading crown to the shrub.

During the summer months the small, round berries change from green to red and, by late August, have reached the bluish-black shade of maturity. They formed a staple diet of the Indians and were used in making pemmican.

For digging sunflower and other roots, the natives made root-diggers from the Saskatoon berry bush. The implements were about 30 inches (75 cm) long with a sharp point at one end and a cross handle at the other. The bush also supplied straight slender stems of hard, fine-grained wood for arrows.

Vancouver 170.1 (274 km) — Kamloops 97.9 (157.5 km)
**Across the river** is a spectacle of mountain scenery that surpasses the average panorama of rugged ridges and steep-walled valleys. Eroding gravel banks rise abruptly from the river and terminate at the edge of gently sloping benches. These, at their higher levels, steepen into crumbling outcroppings which quickly turn into a rocky jumble of cliffs and pinnacles. The light grey rock is broken by irregular bluff patches and zig-zagging white dykes and outcrops. Natural forces have fashioned immense, rocky basins which funnel downward into large gravel flumes. After heavy rainfalls, the water rushes in a mad torrent into these flumes, pulverizing the blocks of eroded rock into gravel.

**Chain mesh** is part of the Highway along here, used to help prevent slides started by rocks rolling down the gravel cuts. The mesh was laid on the theory that stopping rocks from rolling stops the slide from starting. As a bonus it has helped trees and shrubs to take root on the slopes, thus providing even better stability.

Vancouver 171.4 (276 km) — Kamloops 96.6 (155.5 km)
**Here the Highway passes** beneath the CPR tracks and then into what is probably the most sinuous stretch in the nearly 5,000-mile- (8,050-m-) long

In the Fraser Canyon engineers overcame obstacles with a series of tunnels such as Ferrabee, above, but in the Thompson Canyon a different technique was needed. At Nicomen, for instance, the Highway was built right into the river channel because there wasn't room to squeeze it between the CPR and the Thompson.

Trans-Canada Highway. Here the Highway is sandwiched between the rapid-torn Thompson River and the CPR above. In several places it is built into the river channel, supported on steel retaining walls filled with gravel. Rock walls on either side of the river indicate that it has reached its pre-glacial bed and is slowly cutting itself a narrow inner canyon.

**The Steelhead:** In autumn a common sight from here to past Spences Bridge is steelhead fishermen angling for one of North America's most spectacular fish. The steelhead is actually a rainbow trout that spends much of its life in the ocean, returning to fresh water to spawn. Unlike salmon, however, it does not die after spawning but can return time after time, swimming hundreds of miles up the Fraser, Thompson, Skeena and many other rivers to its birthplace. The steelhead is a beautiful silver fish that grows to a generous size, so don't be surprised if a fisherman struggles up the bank to casually display a 25 lb. (11 kg) or larger steelhead. Would-be anglers are reminded to check the regulations carefully since there are both seasonal and area closures on the river. In addition, a special steelhead license is necessary.

**Railroad Construction:** The present CPR line is vastly improved over the original grade. In the 11 miles (17.6 km) between Thompson Siding and Spences Bridge, for instance, there were twenty-two large sections of trestle work. Another 19-mile (30.4-km) stretch of railroad contained thirteen tunnels.

Vancouver 173.7 (280 km) — Kamloops 94.3 (151.5 km)

**Nicomen River and Bridge:** Did this small waterway trigger the Fraser River gold rush of 1858? Indians were the first settlers. Their village was called Nequamin, and the splendid fishing made it a populous place. Coarse gold, in the form of a 3-ounce (85-gram) nugget, was found here in the 1850s by an Indian kneeling to drink. This could have been the incident that resulted in the Fraser River gold rush, although who first found gold on the Mainland and when and where are questions still not satisfactorily answered.

Some say that Chief Trader McLean of the Hudson's Bay Company of Fort Kamloops bought gold from the Indians as early as 1852. Others say that John Houston, a Scottish sailor, first found gold on Tranquille Creek in 1857. Another version, as mentioned above, is that in 1856 an Indian paused on the bank of the Nicomen River for a drink and noticed a yellowish pebble in the gravel. He fished it out and it proved to be gold. Soon the entire tribe was at work recovering the yellow stones and selling them to the Hudson's Bay Company.

Of this latter fact there is no doubt. By February 1858, the Company had 800 ounces (22,640 grams) of gold. It also faced a dilemma. A horde of miners clumping through the wilderness was the last thing the Hudson's Bay Company wanted. Over the years they had built a monopoly in the fur trade and they knew from past experience that newcomers always disrupted this monopoly, with a corresponding drop in Company profits. But Company officers were also practical. The 800 ounces (22,640 grams) of gold was of little commercial value in its raw state. It had first to be minted — and the nearest mint was in San Francisco. Accordingly, in

February 1858 the nuggets and flakes were loaded on the steamer *Otter* for shipment to the mint.

At that time in San Francisco almost anyone of importance belonged to the Volunteer Fire Department, and the mint Superintendent was no exception. At a firemen's meeting shortly after the arrival of the *Otter*, the conversation turned to gold. The Superintendent was present and remarked: "Boys, the next excitement will be on the Fraser River." He then told about the coarse gold which the purser of the *Otter* had brought to the mint.

The Superintendent's prediction proved accurate. As mentioned in the text at Mile 110.3, a small party of miners left San Francisco to explore the Fraser and found gold near Fort Yale. Within months some 30,000 hopeful men stampeded to the river, changing the land forever.

**Jaws of Death** is the appropriate name for the formidable rapids just downstream from the junction of the two rivers. This is one of the areas where the Highway is built into the river channel. In summer commercial firms operate raft tours on both the Thompson and the Fraser Rivers, the motto of passengers seemingly "The rougher the water, the more enjoyable the trip."

Just upstream Nicomen Falls are almost hidden by towering cliffs. The cliffs have a reddish tinge formed by alteration of a volcanic rock called basalt. Great thicknesses of lava have covered most of the Nicomen Plateau and are often of a bubbly nature with the cavities filled by some type of mineral. For mineral collectors, geodes filled or lined with chalcedony, amethystine quartz, opal, and various zeolites may be found in the vicinity.

**For much of the route between Lytton and Spences Bridge the CNR (on the far bank), the Thompson River, the Highway and the CPR (above the Highway), are within shouting distance of each other.**

**The Cariboo Wagon Road** crossed the Nicomen River near its mouth and for years a frame roadside hotel just south of today's railroad underpass provided accommodation for stagecoach passengers and freighters. It was operated by a colorful couple, Art Clements and his wife.

In the rough, boisterous atmosphere of those early days, Mrs. Clements more than stood her own. Once a quarrelsome customer was so forcibly "soothed" that a special train had to be summoned to rush him to hospital in Vancouver. It turned out that she had dealt the telling blow with an earthenware "under-the-bed" accessory — a standard bedroom furnishing of the times.

Vancouver 179.1 (288.3 km) — Kamloops 88.9 (143.2 km)

**Shaw Springs:** Now the site of a resort, this large flat once marked a night's resting place for the sweating mule and bull teams. The number of old oxen and mule shoes found here may indicate it once was a shoeing depot.

Quantities hauled 400 miles (644 km) to the Cariboo from Yale in the covered freight wagons were immense. On September 29, 1868, a merchant named Thos. L. Briggs at Cameronton just down Williams Creek from Barkerville advertised in the *Cariboo Sentinel* that he had ". . . just received . . . 6,000 pounds premium Sumass fresh butter . . . also 3000 Gallons assorted LIQUORS, in case or bulk; 500 Gallons DEVOE'S COAL OIL; 5000 lbs. English, French and American CANDLES; 10 bbls No. 1 Mountain Silver TROUT."

Vancouver 179.9 (289.6 km) — Kamloops 88.1 (141.9 km)

**Gold Pan Provincial Park:** Although it has only 14 campsites and a picnic area, this park with its riverside setting is extremely popular — especially in autumn when the steelhead are running. The main road through the area was part of the original Cariboo Wagon Road.

**Gold Panning:** Along the Thompson River in many areas, colors and even flakes of gold can be found in the gravel bars or near the river's edge. During the Depression years of the 1930s more than 600 men mined the Thompson River between Lytton and Spences Bridge. Their workings, in the form of tailings or piles of boulders, can be seen in many places along the river banks.

**Sidehill Gouger Tracks:** And what is a Sidehill Gouger? Well, see how some of the sidehills show a tracery of horizontal lines, or narrow paths. They are made by that phantom animal, the Sidehill Gouger. Nature has obligingly adapted its anatomy to the steep sidehills by giving the Gouger two shorter legs on one side. Constructed in this peculiar fashion, it walks only on sloping ground, but since it can't turn around, it must continue onward, ever onward.

People who don't believe in such an animal say that the trails are found over much of the Interior grazing region. They point out that cattle prefer to feed with their feet on the level and so, over the course of time, have worn little paths into the grazing slopes. This scientific explanation is given further credibility by the fact that the paths are exactly "the length of a critter's neck apart."

**Groundhogs:** While travellers are unlikely to see a Sidehill Gouger, they may see a groundhog, also known as marmot and woodchuck. Their tunnel entrances are usually near piles of rock which serve as look-outs. The moment they sense that they are under observation, these squat, compact animals scamper for their tunnels. Often beady-eyed individuals are seen standing erect as ramrods, or lying flat on their stomachs, appraising the intruder. One suspicious move and an acrobatic movement almost too quick for the eye puts them in safety. They may be seen here and there along rocky sections of roads throughout the Interior.

The Indians trapped large numbers of them and used ten or twelve skins to make a warm robe. Even now, in certain parts of the Interior, groundhogs are valued as food by the Indians.

Vancouver 182 (293 km) — Kamloops 86 (138.5 km)
**Bighorn Highway Center:** This tourist facility is named after the Rocky Mountain bighorn sheep which inhabit the rugged mountains across the river.

**Anyone Interested in Rattlesnakes?** These heat-loving reptiles are partial to the warm, dry Thompson River Valley, although they are not numerous. The species here is the Pacific rattlesnake, the only poisonous snake in B.C. It grows over 48 inches (125 cm) long and in its general, ground-blending color there are a series of dark brown oval patches down the back. These narrow into crossbars towards the tail. The blotches and the rattle on the end of the tail form unmistakable identifying features. This snake prefers dry, hot areas but evidently can't stand too much direct sunlight, as it is usually found in the shade of sagebrush or rocks. Its food consists of gophers, mice, and other small rodents.

All snakes shed their skin periodically. Shedding starts at the head with the snake becoming partially blind as the skin around the eyes loosens. This is the time the rattlesnake reportedly strikes without warning. When the skin comes loose about the head, the snake crawls out, peeling the skin inside out by catching it on grass or rough ground. A new segment is added to the rattle each time. These additions do not tell the snake's age, however, since skin may be shed twice a year.

**Sagebrush and Rabbit Bush**, two plants common to this region, are sometimes confused by people not familiar with them. Sagebrush is easy to distinguish because of its comparatively large size, twisted and gnarled branch-structure, sage-grey color, and sage-like smell. Each bush is a distinct individual, although further north they grow so thick that a coarse mat effect is produced. Most people won't notice "When the Bloom is on the Sage" for several reasons. It doesn't bloom until October and then the small, inconspicuous yellow flowers usually escape notice.

Rabbit Bush is smaller, more compact and a softer grey than sagebrush. Its tufted heads of small yellow flowers are in bloom during August and September and are a conspicuous distinguishing feature.

Vancouver 185.2 (298.1 km) — Kamloops 82.8 (133.4 km)
**Junction of Highways 1-8 and Stop of Interest:** A GREAT LANDSLIDE: "Suddenly on the afternoon of August 13, 1905, the lower side of the mountain slid away. Rumbling across the valley in seconds, the slide buried alive five Indians and dammed the Thompson River for over four hours. The

Gold Pan Provincial Park on the Thompson River is a year round favorite. The main road through the campsite is part of the original Cariboo Wagon Road.

The sign opposite at Spences Bridge is to protect a band of bighorn sheep.

CAUTION
WATCH FOR
MOUNTAIN SHEEP
ON ROAD
FOR 4 km

WELCOME TO..
SPENCES
BRIDGE

trapped water swept over the nearby Indian village, drowning thirteen persons.''

It was 3:25 p.m., August 13, 1905, when Old Chief Lillooet, revered by the Indians as their wisest counsellor, stepped from his house and walked towards the river. It was nearly train-time and it was one of his delights to stand on the riverbank and watch the huge Mogul engine whiz past at a fast 30 miles (48 km) an hour, dragging its shiny red and black coaches through the winding defiles.

At 3:29, just as the passenger train drew abreast of the Indian village at Spences Bridge, there was a bone-jarring thud, followed by a tremendous roar. The Indians looked toward Arthur Seat Mountain. To their horror they saw the entire side start to move. The rumbling overwhelmed all other sounds as the mass hurtled downwards; ponderous boulders hurtling high into the air, and bouncing far into space. The murderous mass buried alive five inhabitants of the wooden village and trapped others as they fled. Plunging into the river, the slide created a giant wave that raced in both directions. Chief Lillooet was caught in that wave and perished.

Blocked by a mountain of debris, the river rose 10 ft. (3 m) in five minutes. As water rose over the flats, those trapped in the debris were drowned. From their vantage point on the elevated tracks, the train passengers watched — helpless to assist.

Remnants of the slide in the form of 20-30-ft. (6-9-m) vegetation-covered hummocks still dot the flat between the Highway and river. Across the river, partly dwarfed by distance, is the remaining 80-ft.- (25-m-) high tongue of the slide.

**Highway 8 heads 40 miles (65 km)** eastward up the Nicola River to Merritt. It is also part of a loop drive back to Hope via the $250 million Coquihalla Highway. The Indian cemetery at the Junction dates back to the first efforts by the missionaries over a century ago to convert the Indians to using the Christian method of burial.

**Wild Clematis, Virgin's Bower, or Traveller's Joy** is a common climber throughout the Interior where it is seen twined on fences and over shrubs. In the spring it is white, with clusters of small flowers, and later on a white silky mass of fine seeds. Some plants have been known to grow over 40 ft. (12.5 m).

Vancouver 185.6 (298.8 km) — Kamloops 82.4 (132.7 km)
**Thompson River and Bridge:** The river crossing here during the early 1860s was by a ferry on a cable. Known as Cook's Ferry, it was replaced by a $15,000 bridge built by Thomas Spence in 1864. Since Spence was allowed to charge a toll to pay for his bridge, the community became known as Spence's Bridge. Spence became Division Superintendent of the Cariboo Wagon Road and later a prominent citizen in Victoria. In June 1881 he died after falling down a flight of stairs at the city's Angel Hotel.

Vancouver 186.2 (299.8 km) — Kamloops 81.8 (131.7 km)
**Spences Bridge**, area population 300. There are actually two communities, the old and the new. The original community is on the east bank of the Thompson River and dates to the Cariboo gold rush.

The Cariboo Wagon Road entered town on a lower river bench behind the present buildings. The first building of any size was a log hotel erected by Art Clements, the hosteler from the already-mentioned Nicomen River Hotel. Some people had gold fever, but Clements had building fever. Stores and houses rapidly went up under his direction and he soon was comfortably rich. "To everyone's amazement," said an old-timer, "he went to Mexico and read Shakespeare."

When the Trans-Canada Highway was reconstructed during the 1960s the old community was by-passed. The "new" Spences Bridge consists of businesses along the highway to cater to travellers.

**The Aisle of Trees** are graceful locust trees that form an arch over the old road just down from the present Highway. They were planted in 1904 by the first white woman to come to these far-away parts and formed part of the Smith Ranch. In addition, Mrs. Smith planted fruit trees, whose fruit was so perfectly formed that it was displayed at the London Exposition. There it caught the eye of King Edward VII who sent his compliments to the Smiths.

**The Nicola River** joins the Thompson at Spences Bridge. Its wide terraced valley which branches southeasterly was once covered by the tents of Indians who gathered for the fine fishing. Fish were caught from platforms erected on the south side of the river below the mouth of the Nicola. Above this point, they built a weir across the river and speared them by the thousands.

Down the Nicola Valley, in later years, thousands of steers were driven

**Arthur Seat Mountain from the Junction of Highways 1 and 8, with a CNR freight train passing the tongue of the slide which killed thirteen people.**

to market from the large pioneer ranches located in the upper valley. They were then herded down the Cariboo Wagon Road to Yale and loaded on sternwheel steamers.

**CAUTION — Watch for Mountain Sheep on Road:** So say signs at both approaches to Spences Bridge. They really should be amended to read "especially in late winter and spring" since that is when the winter snows drive the bighorn off the mountains to lower elevations and when they are most likely to be seen. This band of Rocky Mountain bighorn are not native to the area but introduced from the Rockies. At one time there were probably over 1 million bighorn sheep in North America. Today there are perhaps 25,000, so drive carefully when the Spences Bridge band is present.

**Northward from Spences Bridge** the Highway climbs onto the Interior Plateau, providing panoramic views of Thompson River Valley and the parched banks and mountains rising from it. On the way are a number of fruit stands with locally grown tomatoes, apples, corn and similar products.

Many of the farms date back to the 1860s when disappointed miners decided that there was more money in tilling the soil than digging the gravel. One of the first places is shown on early maps as the 89-Mile Stable with another reference calling it "French Pete's." It was a half-day's journey from Spences Bridge, in contrast to the few minutes of today.

**Hoodoos** have been sculptured across the river in several locations by the erosive action of wind and rain. In time, the banks will be so traversed by small deep gullies that the knobs, spires and pillars will form miniature badlands.

Vancouver 191.6 (308.5 km) — Kamloops 76.4 (121 km)
**Historic Martel Ranch:** The orchard below the Highway is part of a ranch started in the 1880s by a Frenchman. Little is known of him except that his life's fortune of several thousand dollars was reportedly buried somewhere in the great outdoors.

After twice changing hands, the ranch came into the possession of Joe Martel. Small of stature but big in endeavor, Martel made himself a well known personage. The fine fruit from his orchard was loaded on a wagon and sold along the Cariboo Wagon Road where it found a ready market. The mountain behind the ranch is named after him, as is a station on the railroad.

The orchard is today owned by the Paulos family who in season sell fruit and vegetables at a roadside stand. Several of the pear trees are over 100 years old and still producing.

Vancouver 194.6 (313.4 km) — Kamloops 73.4 (118.1 km)
**Across the Thompson** is an excellent example of a talus slope, so prominent that it was featured on early maps. Some idea of its size can be gained by comparing it with the church on the Indian reserve between the base of the slide and the river. Although the greater part of this mountain is granite, there is a section above the slide of particular interest. It is of volcanic origin, composed of extremely large pieces of ejected material which have been compacted into a jig-saw puzzle of fragments. Some limestone and greenstone fragments are nearly 3 ft. (1 m) in diameter. Most limestone

The prominent talus slope across the Thompson River north of Spences Bridge completely overwhelms the Indian church.

Northward from Spences Bridge the Trans-Canada climbs from water level to the arid sagebrush-covered benchlands of the Interior dry belt.

blocks are dark grey in color, while others have been changed into an attractive white marble. Great chunks have broken away from this upper mass and transferred their particular color to the symmetrically-shaped rockslide below.

The angle, or slope at which the slide lies, is known as the "angle of repose." So delicately balanced is this slope in slides of fine material that the disturbance caused by the pressure of a foot starts the upper section in movement to correct the balance.

Vancouver 197.3 (317.7 km) — Kamloops 70.7 (113.8 km)

**Viewpoint of the Thompson River** and silt cliffs characteristic of the region. During the ice age deep beds of silt were deposited on the bottom of temporary lakes formed by ice dams. When the ice melted the water cut channels through the silt, leaving today's banks and terraces.

Across the river is the station which pumps water some 10 miles (16 km) over the mountains to the Highland Valley copper mine. Copper is common in the area, the greenish tinge on many rock outcrops evidence of the mineral. Other colored rocks are visible on various slopes wherever the thin layer of soil has been eroded. The rock is crushed and shattered into crumbling fragments which impart rich colors of red, yellow, cream, and white to the otherwise drab slopes.

The intense pressures that have altered these one time granites and volcanics to their present crumbling and colorful forms may have accompanied the intrusion of a tremendous mass of granite rock which now stands as an imposing rocky range east of the river. Glossy Mountain, elevation 6,150 ft. (1,845 m), forms the highest point in the range.

Vancouver 198.3 (319.3 km) — Kamloops 69.7 (112.2 km)

**Stop of Interest** — CANADIAN NORTHERN PACIFIC'S LAST SPIKE: "Canada's third trans-continental rail link was completed near Basque on January 23, 1915. In a simple ceremony the last spike was driven, witnessed by a small group of engineers and workmen. The line later became part of the Federal Government's consolidated Canadian National Railways system."

**The Canadian Northern Pacific Railway:** The early 1900s were boom years with hundreds of thousands of immigrants flocking to Western Canada. To the envy of the Grand Trunk Railway which was operating in Ontario, and the Canadian Northern Railway with lines between Ontario and Saskatchewan, the CPR was monopolizing the entire lucrative western trade.

In 1902, the Canadian Northern announced it was extending its lines from coast to coast. The Grand Trunk also made known the same decision. Since the two couldn't agree on consolidation, two parallel lines were built, both funnelling towards the same gap in the rugged barrier of the Rocky Mountains — the Yellowhead Pass. It had been discarded by the CPR but now both railroads squeezed themselves into its narrow confines. From Yellowhead the Grand Trunk Pacific continued across Central B.C. some 700 miles (1,125 km) to a new port called Prince Rupert, while the Canada Northern headed southward 500 miles (805 km) to Vancouver. The GTP was completed in 1914 and the CNR the next year. But by then both lines were in financial trouble, the Grand Trunk's problems made worse because its president and driving force, Charles Hays, had drowned in the *Titanic* disaster.

After World War One both lines were taken over by the Federal government which merged them and other bankrupt lines into Canadian National Railways. All were consolidated and today the CN with a staff of more than 90,000 operates over 34,000 miles (54,750 km) of track and an array of related businesses which include ferries, hotels, and microwave systems.

**The Meandering Thompson River:** Possibly the most striking view of the Thompson is that of its graceful, meandering passage through the white-walled cliffs of its inner valley. Up the valley from the Highway, the winding blue ribbon reaches to the inner vastness of the Interior Plateau.

**Russian thistle, or tumbleweed,** is familiar to most people. While it isn't a true thistle, the other part of its name does have significance. This tumbleweed was introduced from Russia through seed impurities and has spread rapidly over a vast area of North America. It grows as a bushy herb some 12-20 inches (30-35 cm) high and is a mass of soft spiny green stems. In fall the round springy plants break off close to the ground and as tumbling tumbleweeds, go rolling before the wind.

Vancouver 201.1 (323.8 km) — Kamloops 66.9 (107.7 km)
**Side Road to Venables Valley:** From the Highway this road crosses a cattle guard — no, not a cowboy with a six-shooter but a culvert-like arrangement of pipes that cattle won't cross — and heads into ranching country. It is named after Captain Cavendish Venables, a British army officer who settled here in the early 1860s. The road traverses backcountry some 26 miles (41.5 km) to rejoin the Trans-Canada at Spences Bridge. It is an interesting trip for those who want a touch of backwoods driving, although good weather is important, otherwise mud can create problems.

Vancouver 203.4 (327.5 km) — Kamloops 64.6 (104 km)
**Red Hill Rest Area,** with picnic tables and rural toilets. The rich reds and browns which stain the hillsides and gullies are the result of iron compounds weathering from the crumbling rocks.

**Oregon Jack Hill** is another name for Red Hill. "Oregon" Jack was an early character who came from Oregon. His real name was John Dowling and he kept a wayside hostel. A traveller in the 1880s described him as "a vile-looking man, with red face, bald head, and bow legs." His chief notoriety arose from the fact that he hadn't been sober since entering B.C. in 1860. Despite this, or perhaps because of it, he was a pleasant man who made his guests comfortable.

**Cactus and Rock Rose:** In such a dry region, the existence of every plant appears remarkable. These two plants, however, manage very well and display beautiful blooms.

The cactus is the common Interior species of the two cacti found in B.C. Spreading slowly through the drier portions of the province, these cacti are at the outer fringe of their homeland in the central regions of the United States and Mexico. They bloom in June, producing a yellow flower that is near perfection in purity of color. The bulbous and mealy stems are well adapted for storing water and, if it weren't for their threatening spines, they would soon be exterminated by thirsty animals.

Indians had many uses for the cactus. They roasted and ate it, and used heated cacti to help fix the colors they rubbed over their skin to decorate their bodies. In addition, tattooing was done by puncturing their skin with a cactus spike and passing a fine thread, coated with powdered charcoal, under the skin. Indian women made necklaces by threading cactus flowers on bark fiber.

The rock rose, sandhill rose, or bitterroot, is also well-known throughout the arid regions in the United States. Bitterroot is the State flower of Montana and the Bitterroot Mountains are named after this usually inconspicuous plant. In B.C. it is found around Ashcroft and in certain parts of the Okanagan Valley. The flower, rose-colored and about 1.5 inches (3.8 cm) across, appears on barren sidehills during May and June. It has from ten to fifteen petals and lies close to the ground, opening only when the sun is shining. The plant's roots are swollen and cling tenaciously to life in the rocky soil. Although slightly bitter to the taste, they were used extensively by the Indians as food.

Vancouver 204.8 (329.8 km) — Kamloops 63.2 (101.7 km)
**Side Road to Hat Creek Valley:** This road swings westward up Oregon Jack Creek into Upper Hat Creek Valley. It then branches, the northerly fork continuing to Highway 12 which runs from Lillooet to join with the Cariboo Highway about 7 miles (11 km) north of Cache Creek. The other fork heads southward to provide access to the Trans-Canada Highway at Spences Bridge.

Hat Creek Valley has one of the world's largest coal deposits, some 15 billion tons, which B.C. Hydro once planned to mine to fuel a multi-billion dollar thermal generating plant. So advanced were their plans that they spent several hundred thousand dollars buying ranches in the Valley. But B.C. Hydro miscalculated and the extra power is unnecessary. To the satisfaction of many people concerned about acid rain and other pollutants from thermal power plants, the project has been dropped — at least for now.

In addition to its coal deposits, the Hat Creek Valley has a rich ranching heritage. In 1865 the Cornwall Brothers, after using the valley as their private hunting grounds, took out the first homestead. They used the land to graze cattle and grow hay, but then came permanent settlers such as the Parks, Pococks and Lehmans. The Ashcroft Museum has an outstanding display on the history of the Valley.

(Travellers venturing onto Hat Creek or other side roads will find information on maps and guide books at Mile 87.9.)

Vancouver 209.5 (337.3 km) — Kamloops 58.5 (94.2 km)
**Stop of Interest** — ASHCROFT MANOR: "In 1862 C. F. and H. P. Cornwall settled here and developed Ashcroft Manor. The ranch with its grist and saw mills supplied Cariboo miners. The manor house was destroyed by fire in 1943, but the road house survives.

"Clement Cornwall became one of British Columbia's first senators after confederation with Canada in 1871, and Lieutenant-Governor of British Columbia in 1881."

Ashcroft Manor is hidden behind an elm grown from a seed planted over 100 years ago. In addition to being a stopping place with an excellent reputation, the Manor was the district's first courthouse, complete with jail in the cellar.

Behind the Manor is a sod-roofed cabin, below, built in 1863 to provide accommodation for Chinese workers. A creek diverted through the back of the center section made a natural cooler for meat and dairy products.

**Ashcroft Manor** was widely known in stagecoach and freight wagon days, both as Cornwall's and Ashcroft Manor. The Cornwall brothers came from England in 1859, and built Ashcroft Manor in 1862, naming it after their home in England. A primitive flour mill was erected and the flour sold to freighters and miners. At the Manor are the oldest mill stones in B.C. These were carried in by packhorse and used in a mill operating on Cornwall Creek in 1860. One of the earliest water licenses in the province was obtained in 1864 on this same creek.

The first cattle (150 head) were purchased for $10 apiece at Coeur D'Alene, Idaho. Bringing them home "only" entailed a drive across the State of Washington, then some 200 miles (320 km) up the Okanagan Valley, over the hills to a swim across the Thompson River and, finally, into home pasture. The gold rush stimulated sales and the cattle were sold at a good profit.

Two English traditions that the Cornwall brothers maintained over a century ago were horse racing and fox hunting. The horse races on Cornwall Flats attracted upwards of 1,000 spectators from all over B.C., most arriving on horseback or by stagecoach. When English thoroughbreds failed to satisfy the sporting brothers' demands, they imported an Arabian stud. Horse racing died out eventually and the flats later became the first landing field in the Interior.

The fox hunts — actually coyote hunts — were conducted with the same pomp and ceremony as in England. The illusion was heightened by

having Indians dressed in red coats. Their main duty was opening and closing gates as the boisterous hunters charged across farm and field. Every effort was made to procure the best hounds, even to having special dogs shipped around Cape Horn in sailing ships.

In the days when roadside hostels were so rough and dirty that some discerning travellers preferred to sleep in the fields, Cornwall's was described as "the quietest, most comfortable hotel on the road with lots of English papers lying around the rooms." The original building also served as the first courthouse in the area, as well as a store and post office.

The Manor is still serving the public, although not as a hostel. It is now a museum where visitors can turn back the clock well over a century and see how travellers were accommodated in the early 1860s. The two large elms in front of the building were brought as seedlings from England and are now over 100 years old, as is a log building behind the Manor. Operated in conjunction with the Manor are two shops, Manor Arts and Crafts and Roadhouse Collectables which feature B.C. handicrafts and antiques, and Ashcroft Manor Teahouse. In addition to offering a traditional English cup of tea, the Teahouse is licensed and serves full course meals among shade trees which date back to stagecoach days.

Vancouver 209.7 (337.7 km) — Kamloops 58.3 (93.8 km)
**Ashcroft Junction (South):** Here a paved highway loops 9 miles (14.4 km) through Ashcroft and rejoins the Trans-Canada 4 miles (6.4 km) to the north. From Ashcroft another paved highway heads southeast to the mining region of Highland Valley and Logan Lake, and is an alternate paved route to Kamloops and to Hope via Merritt and the Coquihalla Highway.

**Freight wagons leave Ashcroft for the Cariboo in the 1890s. The community is proud of its history, with its museum one of the most interesting in B.C.**

**Signs of the Big Slide of 1880** can be glimpsed down-river from vantage points on the twisting road. The slide remants take the form of hoodoos, or pinnacles, along the broken front of the whitish bluffs.

This slide occurred much the same way as the 1905 one at Spences Bridge. A huge section of escarpment tumbled into the river, forming a dam. The imprisoned waters covered the river terraces on which Ashcroft was later built. In those days, a flour mill stood at the mouth of Bonaparte River which joins the Thompson about a mile (1.6 km) above town. The flood waters climbed higher and higher, finally stopping at the mill sign nailed half way up the building. A picture of the mill is on display in the Ashcroft Museum, as is the actual sign.

**Ashcroft**, area population 5,500, is a modern community with most visitor services and a peaceful setting on the east bank of the Thompson River. Between the building of the Cariboo Wagon Road in 1863 and the construction of the CPR in 1882-85, the stopping place for traffic was Cornwall's Ranch. Then, as the grade for the railroad forged ahead, Ashcroft was born and became a depot point. For a time it was called Ashcroft Station because the Cornwalls resented the name of Ashcroft being used for any place but the Manor.

With the completion of the railway, Ashcroft replaced Yale as "The Gateway to the Cariboo." Through Ashcroft until 1916, when the government-owned Pacific Great Eastern Railway was finished, the entire flow of goods and freight moved to and from the sprawling ranch lands of the Cariboo and Chilcotin, the Barkerville goldfields, and into Central B.C. Ashcroft was the only shipping point for the thousands of cattle that were raised in the rolling grazing lands stretching northward for over 200 miles (322 km). Here, too, came the bags of gold dust so dramatically won from the rivers and creeks.

This history comes alive at the Ashcroft Museum, one of the most interesting in B.C. It was founded by R. D. Cumming in 1935 and housed over the offices of the *Ashcroft Journal* which he ran. In 1958 Cumming died and a museum built in his name opened the same year. The original collection has since been expanded by many donations from the community and the Museum moved into a two-story former government building.

The lower floor exhibits portray the history of Southern Cariboo and the Indians tribes who first settled the area. There are replicas of early stores, scores of artifacts and an excellent collection of photos which vividly illustrate life as it was between the first settlement in 1883 and the great fire which destroyed much of the downtown core in 1916.

The top floor is dedicated to the history of the Upper Hat Creek Valley. Both the coal mining and ranching exhibits are excellent, the latter told through the words and photos of families still living in the area.

One pioneer, Johnny Morgan, recalled haying time on a ranch — always a hectic race to beat bad weather. "Hell, we were chocking up hay there just almost on the run," he remembered. "I said 'What kind of goddarn hay you putting up here? Is it all wild? By the way you boys are running after it, you'd think it was'."

**Dry Belt Desolation:** Although there are other arid portions of B.C. in the southern Okanagan and Similkameen Valleys, few places impart such an atmosphere of desolation as the parched terrain along the non-irrigated section of the loop from Ashcroft to its northern junction with the Trans-Canada. Here annual precipitation is only 7 inches (18 cm) and the hardy cactus and sagebrush appear to wither in their struggle for survival. Above, the bare black mountains brood in funereal silence, the folds and wrinkles in their skin further accentuating the impression of a land just taken from some huge oven.

Vancouver 213.4 (343.6 km) — Kamloops 54.6 (87.9 km)
**Ashcroft Junction (North):** Here a paved road loops 9 miles (14.4 km) through Ashcroft and rejoins the Trans-Canada 4 miles (6.4 km) to the south. From Ashcroft another paved highway heads southeast to the mining region of Highland Valley and Logan Lake, providing an alternate paved route to Kamloops and to Hope via Merritt and the Coquihalla Highway.

Vancouver 216.1 (347.9 km) — Kamloops 51.9 (83.6 km)
**Cache Creek and Junction of Highways 1-97:** Highway 97 heads northward for some 2,300 miles (3,700 km) via the Cariboo, Central B.C. and Peace River Country through the Yukon to Fairbanks, Alaska. At Prince George it joins Highway 16 which threads across Central B.C. some 500 miles (805 km) west to Prince Rupert and 240 miles (386 km) east to Jasper, then across the prairies.

Since Cache Creek is virtually totally dependant on travellers, its business places include many service stations, motels, and restaurants. There are several versions of how its name originated. One is that in the 1850s a man named Cache lived on the small creek. But because nobody seems to know anything else about Mr. Cache, this is probably more myth than fact. Another theory is that some desperados robbed a pack train of its gold, cached the treasure, but all died one way or the other before recovering it and the treasure is still "cached." While this version has a decided Wild-West flavor, it also appears to be a myth and has little support from historians.

The most logical reason for the name was advanced by historian-newspaperman R. D. Cumming. In the *Ashcroft Journal*, June 18, 1953, he wrote:

"The Hudson's Bay Company was the first business enterprise to open up a branch at Cache Creek. They built a store that has since been torn down. They founded Cache Creek many years before the Cariboo mining excitement in the 1860s, and they were occupied in bringing furs of all kinds via pack train from the north to their headquarters at Kamloops. They were mostly of French descent, and since 'Cache' is of French origin, it is most likely the settlement was named by them, as a place where they cashed in furs on the way south and obtained food, groceries, etc. on the way north."

**At Cache Creek** the Trans-Canada Highway changes direction from northward to eastward, but still traverses dry-belt country. In fact, this region is a tongue of the Sonoran Desert which angles northwestward from Mexico through the Okanagan Valley to Kamloops, then westward to the Lillooet area and south to the junction of the Thompson-Fraser Rivers at Lytton.

Bonaparte House at Cache Creek in the 1860s, typical of the log-built stopping places along the 400-mile (640-km) Cariboo Wagon Road from Yale to Barkerville.
Below: At Cache Creek the Trans-Canada turns eastward for Kamloops and the Rockies.

**SOME BIRDS TO WATCH FOR:** Without going to any special effort, travellers will probably notice several species of birds, either by reason of their distinctive plumage or some characteristic behavior:

**The magpie** is a large, black and white bird with a graceful tail longer than its body. These features are so distinctive that it cannot be mistaken for another.

**The kingbird**, about two-thirds the size of a robin, is often seen perched on telephone wires along the road. Its motionless, upright posture is similar to that of the flycatcher. The kingbird's darting movements in search of insects and its return to the same perch are other identifying features.

**The red-shafted flicker and Lewis's woodpecker** are both fairly common in this region. The former bird, with its orange colorings under the wing and black bar across a spotted breast, is well known to most people. Its heavy, undulating flight is also a characteristic feature. The Lewis's woodpecker is unusual in coloring. What other bird can match the almost fuchsia of its breast and cheek patches? Otherwise, it is a blackish bird with a restless disposition, evidenced by its short, sporadic flights.

**The bluebirds — Eastern, Western and Mountain** — are all summer residents and easily recognized.

Vancouver 217.6 (350.3 km) — Kamloops 50.4 (81.2 km)
**The Cut-off Valley Road** branches off to the northeast and after approximately 14 miles (22.4 km) meets the Deadman River Valley. This valley can be followed southward to the main highway at Mile 235.6 (379.3 km). Although the road is "country style," it makes an off-the-track alternative that will appeal to the exploring motorist.

Vancouver 218.3 (351.4 km) — Kamloops 49.7 (80.1 km)
**The Semlin Ranch** was established over a century ago by Charles Augustus Semlin. The character and determination of many of these early settlers is indicated by their rise to political prominence. Clement Cornwall, of Cornwall's Lodge less than 10 miles (16 km) from here, was Lieutenant-Governor of the province from 1881 to 1886. Charles Semlin became provincial premier and held office from 1898 to 1900.

Vancouver 220.5 (355 km) — Kamloops 47.5 (76.5 km)
**The Perry Ranch** was pioneered at the same time as Semlin's. To the north escarpments form a massive and colorful wall, the rock split into fissures and caves reminiscent of Western movie settings.

These Tertiary rocks represent a period of prolonged and violent volcanic activity. Behind them a vast irregular plateau stretches into the Cariboo district beyond Clinton. The whole area has been covered with tremendous horizontal lava flows. Prior to these flows the drainage of the Interior Plateau was probably north instead of south since the general elevation is higher in the south than in the north.

Vancouver 225.5 (363 km) — Kamloops 42.5 (68.5 km)
**Here, almost a century ago**, were the headquarters of a ranch owned by John Wilson, the "Cattle King of British Columbia." A Yorkshireman by

birth, Wilson was only seventeen when he immigrated to the United States in 1851. After several years' ramblings, he arrived in British Columbia and tried mining and trading along the Fraser River and in the Cariboo. Although these ventures proved unprofitable, he did become adept at cards. He probably could have made a good living as a professional poker player and faro dealer had he not become interested in the cattle business.

This small ranch, pre-empted in 1860 by two Frenchmen, was bought by Wilson and became famous as 8-Mile Creek, or the "Home Ranch." Wilson ran up to 5,000 head of cattle and utilized other places at Walhachin, Copper Creek and Westholme. His name was a legend throughout the province. Tragically, he died in 1904 after being thrown from his buggy, leaving a wife and nine children. He is buried with many other pioneers in a little cemetery across the west end of Kamloops Lake.

Vancouver 226.3 (364.3 km) — Kamloops 41.7 (67.2 km)
**Stop of Interest** — GHOST OF WALHACHIN: "Here bloomed a 'Garden of Eden'! The sagebrush desert changed to orchards through the imagination and industry of English settlers during 1907-14. Then the men left to fight — and die — for king and country. A storm ripped out the vital irrigation flume. Now only ghosts of flume, trees, and homes remain to mock this once thriving settlement."

**The Tragedy of Walhachin:** Sagebrush! Sagebrush! Thousands of these coarse grey bushes cover the wide benches along the road. And what use are they with their warped stems and pungent smell? But, if they were only apple trees — that would be a sight to see! Such were the thoughts of an enterprising American, C. E. Barnes, as he gazed over the drab expanse of old river terraces that stretched far back on either side of the river.

At Barnes' instigation a British company bought a local ranch called Pennie's in 1908. A new company, The British Columbia Horticultural Estate, was formed which purchased the surrounding land until it owned over 5,000 acres (2,030 ha). The company's plan was to irrigate the land, plant fruit trees and then sell the property.

With Barnes as manager, it was decided that the irrigation water would come from the Deadman Creek drainage. In 1910 a dam was built on Snohoosh (Deadman) Lake. Then came the gigantic task of building a ditch and flume to the orchard sites. In all, precious waters were carried 20 miles (32 km) in a 6-ft.- (2-m-) wide ditch and across the high ravines and rocky hillsides in a wooden flume supported on trestlework.

With the irrigation problem solved, the sagebrush was quickly uprooted by a ponderous steam tractor and plow unit. Healthy, young apple trees were set out in neat rows. Under the magic touch of water, the soil released its riches. The formerly arid wastes were quickly transformed into a green carpet of cover-crops, criss-crossed by the neat rows of thousands of apple trees.

A promotional plan to settle these lands was instigated by the company. The inducements sound fabulous when compared with present-day values. Planted orchard land was offered for sale at $350 per acre, while four-room houses with bath were listed at $1,100, additional rooms estimated to cost $125 apiece. A modern hotel, golf course, monorail

At Walhachin, water brought 7 miles (11 km) in a massive main flume was the key to growing both fruit and vegetables. The man at the base of the trestle gives an indication of some of the work necessary to transform the land from sagebrush to gardens and orchards.

transportation system, football field, tennis courts, and skating rink were some of the facilities planned for Walhachin.

Families from England were encouraged to immigrate and Walhachin developed as a center of cultural and fashionable living. The company erected a fine hotel and started a packing house to prepare the fruit for shipping. By 1913, the once dry and desolate wastes were a picture of productive beauty. The town was growing rapidly with the addition of a number of large houses. The irrigation system was an engineering success and even the benches across the river were getting their share of water from a large pipeline hung across the valley by means of cables.

Barnes had interested the wealthy Marquis of Anglesey in Walhachin. The Marquis, after making heavy investments in the project, moved out from England and built a beautiful home. Long before Hollywood movie stars found out about private swimming pools, he was sporting the real thing in his landscaped grounds.

But the peaceful tenor of this remarkable project was not to continue for long. In 1914, World War One started and the call went out for men. It was then that Walhachin set a record for enlistment that was not surpassed by any village, town, or community in the world. Out of a total male population of 107, 97 went to war. Among those who remained, enthusiasm for the project waned. Then a heavy cloudburst washed away great sections of the flume. The Marquis of Anglesey had, by this time, spent over $1,500,000 and was close to his financial limit. It is reported that he aproached the government to provide half the cost of repairs but was refused.

With almost equal rapidity to that which transformed the barren waste to thriving orchards, the reverse process began. One by one, and then in hundreds, the trees blighted and died. The remaining flumes fell apart and sagebrush crept from the base of the mountain to return as master of the soil.

To see what is left of Walhachin is like viewing the weathered headstone for a once-great man. How can a few dried sticks of apple trees among the sagebrush portray the original panorama of healthy green orchards? The flumes are now a patchwork of boards clinging to rocky slopes. Even Anglesey's fine house has gone.

But what of the future? Will apple trees again clothe these flats in a small-scale imitation of the Okanagan Valley? Probably not. Ironically, the area has proved too cold to grow apples commercially and irrigated hay fields now predominate. Most of the original houses at Walhachin have been torn down and only a remnant community remains.

Vancouver 230.5 (371.1 km) — Kamloops 37.5 (60.4 km)
**Side Road to Walhachin**: It is 4 miles (6.4 km) to the once flourishing community. From the bridge over the Thompson River is an extremely fine view both up and down river. The flats across the Thompson offer an unusual contrast. Green orchards and farms flank the road and yet, not far distant, are moving sand dunes.

On the rock bluff to the north of the Trans-Canada Highway the remains of the old flume can still be seen. In all, it parallels the Highway for some 4 miles (6.4 km). A few scattered skeletons of dead or dying apple trees stand forlornly among the cover of grey sagebrush.

112

Vancouver 235.6 (379.3 km) — Kamloops 32.4 (52.2 km)

**Deadman Creek, or Vidette, Side Road:** This is the eastern section of the loop mentioned at Mile 217.6 (350.3 km). This lower canyon-like appearance is very deceptive for the valley widens in its upper reaches into a farming district. Some 9 miles (14.4 km) up the valley is a spectacular mountainside of colored rock. Beyond this a further 28 miles (45 km) is Deadman River Falls, one of the more scenic waterfalls in the province.

The Deadman Road also gives access to several fishing lakes, including Mowitch, Snohoosh and Vidette. It is also part of a backroad drive over the Tranquille Plateau to Kamloops. A word of caution, however, to those planning to venture onto local byways. If you do not have local knowledge, a detailed map is advisable since there are a maze of logging roads throughout the area. It is easy to get lost and there are no gas stations.

At Mile 87.9 (141.6 km) we mentioned sources of maps and guide books for side roads in the Lower Mainland and west of the Trans-Canada Highway. Here are some commercial publications that will aid visitors to this area — especially those who intend to fish any of the scores of lakes for which the Kamloops region is famous:

*Outdoor Recreation Maps of British Columbia:* This series of maps is published by the Outdoor Recreation Council of B.C. Number 4 covers the Greater Kamloops Region and shows roads, trails, points of interest, boat launching sites, campgrounds and similar information.

*Fishing and Hunting Map of South Central B.C.:* Published by the Kamloops and District Fish and Game Association, this map shows roads — including logging roads and jeep trails — fishing resorts, public and private campsites and similar data of interest to fishermen and hunters.

*Thompson-Kamloops-Nicola Fishing Guide:* This is a comprehensive guide to lakes and rivers from Lytton on the Trans-Canada Highway to the Kamloops area, and includes the Southern Cariboo and southward to Merritt and the Nicola Valley. Contains maps and an excellent description of lakes, their fish and their facilities, as well as tips for anglers.

*Okay Anglers Fishing Directory & Atlas:* This book provides specific information on some 2,000 lakes and streams in B.C. Includes many maps in four-color and articles on flies, tackle tips and a centerfold index of over 4,000 listings of rivers and lakes.

*Fishing Guide to Fresh Water in British Columbia:* A directory of some 2,000 lakes and rivers with information on how to get there, facilities and species of fish. Also contains fishing tips and other features of interest to the fresh-water fisherman.

These publications are generally available at newsstands, sporting goods stores and similar outlets.

Vancouver 236.5 (380.7 km) — Kamloops 31.5 (50.8 km)

**Deadman River and Bridge:** Many years ago an Indian found an outcrop of ore-bearing rock far up Deadman River. Attaching little importance to it, he sold the information and samples to the postmaster at Savona for $10. This gentleman couldn't stir up enough enthusiasm to investigate; he made a tidy profit of $5 by selling his knowledge to another for $15. Finally, the Vidette Mine was founded — and yielded about one million dollars in gold.

The Thompson River between Savona and Spences Bridge flows through country typical of the dry belt — sagebrush, sand cliffs and, opposite page, erosion pillars.

Vancouver 238 (383.1 km) — Kamloops 30 (48.4 km)
**Side Road to Copper Creek:** This route provides another back road drive to Kamloops via the Tranquille Plateau. Before setting out, however, visitors should read the advice on maps and guides books at Mile 235.6 (379.3 km).

Vancouver 238.7 (384.3 km) — Kamloops 29.3 (47.2 km)
**Thompson River and Bridge** and the western end of Kamloops Lake. The original crossing here was by a cable ferry.

**Savona's Ferry:** The 1860s trail from Cache Creek closely followed the present Highway, but because there was no bridge crossing at the foot of Kamloops Lake a ferry service was maintained. Connections were made to Kamloops and Shuswap Lake by sternwheel steamers.

The ferry was established in 1859 by a man who remains something of a mystery. He has been referred to as an Italian named Savona and a Frenchman called Francois Saveneux. But whatever his nationality, the ferry became known as Savona. Its owner, however, did not operate it for long. He died in 1862 and was buried on the hill south of the ferry.

A road was completed to the crossing from Cache Creek in 1866 and in the next few years the government operated the ferry. On several occasions the swift current snapped the ferry cables, and in 1879 a passenger was drowned. In 1884 the first bridge was built at a cost of $15,250, but

was swept away in the flood of 1894. Another bridge was opened in 1906 but part of it washed away in 1908. It was rebuilt, then in 1929 replaced by a fourth one, this time at a cost of $180,000. In 1956 the current bridge was built, close to the location of the original one of 1884.

Vancouver 241.6 (388.9 km) — Kamloops 26.4 (42.6 km)
**Exit to the wayside community of Savona and Savona Provincial Park** on the shore of Kamloops Lake with picnicking and swimming facilities.

The original community of Savona was on the north side of the lake but when the CPR reached the present townsite in the winter of 1884-85 the town was literally hauled across the frozen lake. By July 1885 Savona had expanded so much that the CPR proposed re-naming it in honor of Sir William Cornelius Van Horne, the company's first chairman and second president. It is reported, however, that when the august gentleman saw the sprawling collection of shacks and tents about to bear his name, he made it firmly understood that he preferred the community to retain its original name of Savona.

Vancouver 241.9 (389.4 km) — Kamloops 26.1 (42.1 km)
**Road to Highland Valley and Tunkwa and Leighton Lakes:** The lakes are 14 miles (22.4 km) to the south. Both have Forest Service recreation sites and boat launching, and are good for fly fishing.

Non-fishermen, however, can also enjoy the lakes since they abound with wildlife. Here are a few species:

**Killdeer Plovers** with their plaintiff "killdeer" cry, double breast bands and white-banded wings, nest at many lakes.

**The Greater Yellow Legs and Spotted Sandpiper** dabble at the water's edge. The former is the larger of the two and has a long thin beak and bright yellow legs. The sandpiper can be immediately recognized by its constant bobbing up and down. Its movements come as close to being perpetual motion as is possible for a bird. During summer months its breast is covered with distinctive spots.

**Mallards, Pintails, Barrow's Golden Eye, Shovellers, and Ruddy Ducks** are a few ducks which nest in the area. At least twenty-three species pass through this region on their seasonal migrations. Whistling swans and Canada geese are also present, as are loons, osprey and eagles.

**Coots** are the small, black duck-like birds with a white bill that pump their head back and forth when swimming. They inhabit nearly all the small lakes, and borders of many of the larger lakes throughout the province.

**Brewer's, Yellow-headed and Red-winged Blackbirds** are found in the thick mat of bulrushes which frequently grow along the side of lakes. Their noisy arguing continues undiminished throughout the day. Brewer's blackbird is entirely black except for its white eyes. The coloring of the others are as indicated by their names.

**Muskrats** often inhabit the smaller lakes and ponds. Sometimes referred to as the "little cousin of the beaver," the muskrat is a much nearer relative of the meadow mouse. The muskrat secretes a musky odor from well-developed glands — hence its name. When they are present a minutes' quiet observation will usually reveal a moving "V" in the water, or a round ball of fur perched on a mound it has constructed in the lake or pond.

Vancouver 246.2 (396.4 km) — Kamloops 21.8 (35.1 km)
**Kamloops Lake Rest Area** with rural toilets and picnic tables on a lofty viewpoint overlooking Kamloops Lake and a Stop of Interest plaque.

The City of Kamloops is at the eastern end of the lake. A stock and saddle trail, used by the first settlers and travellers over a century ago, stands out across the lake as a light-colored scar on the lower slopes.

Almost directly opposite is Copper Creek, named for the deposits of native copper. The creek is remarkable for the variety of minerals that occur in the varied, colorful and much decomposed rocks. At one time mercury mines, the largest producers in the British Empire, were located at cinnabar deposits on Copper Creek.

**Stop of Interest** — STEAMBOAT SAGA: "Smooth rivers and great lakes once were the highways of travel. On them plied stately paddle-wheelers, helping exploration and settlement of the Interior. They speeded gold-seekers bound for the 'Big Bend' rush of 1864-65. They freighted grain from the Okanagan. They were vital in building the C.P.R. — and doomed by the railway they helped to build."

**Sternwheel Days:** After the 1860s gold rush the vast area between Kamloops, Shuswap Lake and the Northern Okanagan was a roadless wilderness. Until completion of the Canadian Pacific Railway in 1885, main access was by the flat-bottomed sternwheel steamers. From 1866 when the first stern-wheeler, the *Marten*, was launched on Little Shuswap Lake and sailed to Savona where her engines were installed, until the *C.R. Lamb* was beached at Kamloops in 1948, over a dozen sternwheelers plied the inland waterway.

The *Marten*, built by the Hudson's Bay Company to take advantage of the 1866 gold rush to the "Big Bend" of Columbia River, had a short career. Within months the gold rush became known as the "Big Bilk" and collapsed. The *Marten* was tied up at Fort Kamloops where she remained for years, a constant worry to HBC clerk John Tait. In 1874 he wrote to his superiors: "The steamer *Marten* is alright at present. She is pumped out occasionally. I find the greatest danger is when the ice is breaking up . . . on two occasions last spring we had great difficulty keeping her afloat."

The second sternwheeler to appear was the *Kamloops*, built in 1872 by pioneer businessman John Adams. She was a small vessel with a one-man crew and a four-horsepower engine from an 1867 flour mill. The modest vessel, which could sail in 8 inches (20 cm) of water, nevertheless proved quite successful. In 1872 the *New Westminster Mainland Guardian* noted: "She took a large and fashionable party of excursionists on Sunday last, from Savona's Ferry. She will prove a real boon to the farmers and traders in the vicinity."

In 1874 she carried the first white woman settler into the North Okanagan via Shuswap Lake and the Spallumcheen River. She was Mrs. A. L. Fortune, and in her honor the vessel arrived at Fortune's Landing (today's Enderby) with "whistle blowing and the Union Jack and Stars and Stripes flying."

The most impressive sternwheeler to ply Kamloops waters was the *Peerless*, launched in November 1880 by the Kamloops Steam Navigation Company. A few days later the *Victoria Colonist* reported:

"The steamer *Peerless* . . . is as regards speed and draft, the most successful boat of her class yet built in the province."

She was 131 feet (39.8 m) long, with 16 watertight compartments and powerful engines that drove her at 18 knots. With stores and fuel aboard, she required water only 18 inches (45 cm) deep. In June 1881, she sailed over 100 miles (160 km) up North Thompson River, then later that month ventured down the Thompson to Spences Bridge with flour for CPR construction crews. On her return only Captain Irving's skill prevented her from being wrecked. She was five days fighting rocks and rapids in Black Canyon, a stretch of river among the most dangerous in the province.

In 1894 the *Queen* was launched but she had a short career and caused the only fatalities of the sternwheel era. On July 6 her boiler blew up, killing two of her crew. One of those who survived was J. E. Saucier, her owner. He was lying on a mattress when the explosion occurred and was blown out of the vessel on to the lake, the mattress still under him. The Kamloops newspaper reported:

"He instinctively rubbed the soot and ashes from his eyes, and beheld a sight he could not describe. There were the bodies of the others just falling amid a shower of wood and debris of the boat. He was much excited and knew not what to do, but scrambled to get on the largest part of the boat he could see floating and to assist the other men."

The last sternwheeler to ply the Kamloops-Thompson-Shuswap was the *C.R. Lamb*. She was built in 1907 for the Arrow Lakes Lumber Company and described as having "... exceedingly pretty lines for a sternwheeler." But by now roads were linking the various communities along the lakes, there was less and less freight and the sternwheelers disappeared. Finally, only the *C.R. Lamb* remained. She was apparently also destined to join the others but in 1933 was purchased by Captain William Louie, a Kamloops businessman of Chinese descent.

For twenty-five years Captain Louie operated the vessel, carrying cordwood, hay, excursion parties and anything else that brought in revenue. But he was only delaying the inevitable. In 1948 the *C.R. Lamb* was beached near Kamloops and in 1956 Captain Louie died, severing the last link with paddlewheel days. In the Kamloops Museum are preserved a few remnants of the vessel, including her anchor, whistle, helm, Captain Louie's master's certificate, and a model built by S. B. Brooke.

Vancouver 253 (407.3 km) — Kamloops 15 (24.2 km)
**Cherry Creek Ranch,** originally known as Roper's Ranch, is among the district's pioneer cattle ranches. At one time it was called Heron's Ranch and served as headquarters for the largest sheep operation in B.C.

**The Shuswap pocket gopher** is responsible for the small mounds of earth in the scattered fields along the Highway. This seldom seen animal gets the

Kamloops Lake from a Highway viewpoint and, opposite page, sternwheel steamers at Kamloops in 1885. The vessels served the Kamloops-Shuswap region for over 75 years.

name from its large fur-lined cheek pockets which are well developed to meet its strange feeding habits. With its strong foreclaws, the gopher constructs a labyrinth of tunnels to reach its feeding grounds. Earth is pushed out of short inclined tunnels and side tunnels are used to reach edible plants. The gopher keeps the entrances plugged with dirt to prevent snakes from entering, a sensible precaution.

Although much of its food comes from underground roots and bulbs, it does feed at the mouth of the burrow. Only the front of the animal protrudes from the hole and so cautious is it about making this modest appearance that the vegetation is cut quickly and stuffed into cheek pockets for later consumption.

Since the diameter of the tunnels is scarcely larger than the body-diameter of the gopher and there are few "turn-arounds," it is evident that it must travel backwards almost as easily as forwards. Although no one has observed a gopher travelling in such fashion, it is believed that the stout tail, covered with spiny hairs, is used as a feeler when the animal is in "reverse."

MORE SNAKES: The rattlesnake is described at Mile 182 (293 km), but several other species are mentioned here to round out the picture. None is poisonous and, if regarded without the usual prejudiced hysteria, can be as interesting as any of the smaller wild creatures.

**The Rubber snake, or Rubber Boa,** is a relative of the boa constrictor of far-away lands. It has a thick, short body with a blunt tail which, when

raised, can be mistaken for its head. No wonder some people believe they are suffering from sunstroke when they see this two-headed snake. Because it lives much of its life underground the Rubber snake isn't often seen. Its food is made up of mice, small animals, and birds which it crushes to death in true constrictor fashion.

**Western Blue Racer:** Sometimes called Yellow-Bellied Racer, this long, slender snake crawls with its head well off the ground. Brush or shrubs are no obstacle to its rapid progress as it whips through them with amazing speed.

**The Bull snake, or Gopher snake,** grows up to 6 ft. (2 m) long and is the largest snake in B.C. Its back is colored much like a rattlesnake with a series of dark brown patches, but the under surface is very pale with black or brown spots. For food it favors gophers, but many other small rodents and birds' eggs probably make the long, winding, one-way trip. One bull snake was observed almost too bloated to move, its middle section distended to about twice the diameter of a milk tin. To a bull snake, there is no such thing as "its eyes being too big for its stomach."

**Garter snakes** are those colorful individuals with a yellow, orange, or brick-red stripe down their back. The Wandering Garter snake is the one most likely to be found in this region. It is a good swimmer and usually won't be found very far from water. When cornered, its forked tongue flicks in and out like a bright, miniature lightning flash. It will strike fiercely if tormented and the larger snakes can inflict a painful wound. Garter snakes feed on a wide variety of such things as slugs, fish, snails, earthworms, frogs, toads, and mice.

All snakes have a special swallowing apparatus, otherwise some meals would literally split their skulls. The small bones that make up the jaws, front and back, are hinged with elastic ligaments that give great freedom of action and independence of motion to each side of the jaw. The jaw on one side of the prey is inched foward, then the other side takes a step. The needle-shaped teeth, which project backward, keep a firm grip on what progress has been made while the jaws are walked ahead again. In such a fashion, the snake actually surrounds the victim and forces it into its elastic framework.

Vancouver 259.5 (417.8 km) — Kamloops 8.5 (13.7 km)
**Afton Copper Mine and Smelter:** This mine and three others to the southwest in the highly mineralized Highland Valley employ some 2,000 people. Evidence of this mineralization is alkali, the white, pasty substance that fringes some of the lakes and ponds bordering the Highway.

**The alkali** waters of ponds contain quantities of salts leached from the surrounding hills. These salts are deposited as the water evaporates and, united with oils and fats, form soap. It is only in areas of scant rainfall that conditions are favorable for the forming of alkali lakes and flats.

**Sea blight and glasswort** are the peculiar, low reddish-colored plants growing just above the edge of the alkali line. They are fleshy plants with scales taking the place of leaves. Their existence in earth composed almost solely of alkaline salts is a remarkable example of plant adaption to a particular environment. They may be used as indicators as to whether water is alkaline or not. In early days these plants were burnt and the ash, which contains sodium carbonate, formed the soda ash for industrial and commercial use.

**Vancouver 260.7 (419.7 km) — Kamloops 7.3 (11.8 km)**
**Junction of Highways 1-5:** As this book went to press, work was underway on a four-lane super highway from here southward some 125 miles (200 km) through Merritt to Hope. The $375 million project will by-pass the Fraser Canyon and cut driving time to Vancouver by over one hour. It will be a toll highway with proposed charges $8 for private vehicles and $40 for commercial.

The first section — 71.5 miles (115 km) from Hope to Merritt — is scheduled for completion in the summer of 1986, and the Merritt section to this Junction in late 1987 or early 1988. Another section from Merritt to Peachland in the Okanagan is planned but probably will not be completed until 1988 or later.

(See Heritage House book, *Coquihalla Highway and the Nicola Valley*, scheduled for release early in 1987.)

**Vancouver 262.7 (422.9 km) — Kamloops 5.3 (8.6 km)**
**Junction:** Here a paved road heads 15 miles (24 km) to Lac Le Jeune then through the Highland Valley to Logan Lake. At Logan Lake it forks, one branch leading to Ashcroft on the Trans-Canada Highway and the other to Merritt and the four-lane Coquihalla Highway to Hope.

**Lac Le Jeune Provincial Park:** A major development on a lake famous for its rainbow trout. The Park includes 114 campsites, picnic facilities, boat launching ramp and swimming. In winter this area is popular with cross-country skiers, with some 38 miles (60 km) of trails through the rolling rangelands. There is also a lodge on the lake which caters to the public.

**Mariposa lilies** grow rather sparingly throughout the arid benches and slopes. Although possessing a beautiful purple or lavender-colored bloom, their blending with other ground plants makes them inconspicuous. The Mariposa lily measures about 2 inches (5 cm) across and is supported by a stout stem. It has only one basal leaf.

**Vancouver 265.6 (427.6 km) — Kamloops 2.4 (3.9 km)**
**Junction of Highways 1-5:** Until the new Highway described at Mile 260.7 (419.7 km) is completed this is the route to Highway 3 via Merritt, 58 miles (93 km) and Princeton, 116 miles (187 km). The highway is paved and a pleasant drive through ranching country of rolling hills. For the fisherman there are a host of lakes famous for rainbow trout.

Nicola Lake some 45 miles (72.5 km) to the south is the largest and the site of Monck Provincial Park. Beautifully situated overlooking the lake, it has 71 campsites, picnicking area, launching ramp, sani-station, hiking trails, and fishing and swimming.

**Vancouver 266.3 (428.7 km) — Kamloops 1.7 (2.8 km)**
**Junction:** Continue straight ahead on the Trans-Canada bypass for Banff and Highway 5 to Jasper, turn down Columbia Street for Kamloops city center.

One of B.C.'s largest cities, Kamloops has all tourist facilities and is renowned for its Kamloops trout in some 200 lakes within a 75-mile (120-km) radius.

Vancouver 268 miles (431.5 km) — Kamloops 0 miles (0 km)
**Kamloops**, population 67,000. One of B.C.'s largest cities, Kamloops' growth from a small trading post to a modern metropolis has involved all the adventurous phases that could possibly visit any community. Fur traders, gold miners, ranchers, steamboaters, and railway construction gangs, to name but the highlights of endeavor, have added their impetus to this pleasant area of benchland.

The first white man to arrive here was David Stuart, an employee of the Pacific Fur Company with headquarters at Astoria, near the mouth of the Columbia River. Coming northwards on an exploratory trip up the Okanagan Valley in 1811, he quickly assessed the merits of this waterway junction. Right behind him came Alexander Ross, representing the Northwest Company. He, too, was greatly impressed by this, as he noted, "place called by the Indians, Cumloops," meaning "the meeting of the waters."

The exploratory trips having proven highly satisfactory, Stuart returned the following year and built Fort Kamloops on the sandspit between the North and South Thompson Rivers.

A year later, the Company amalgamated with the Northwest Fur Company and, in 1821, this union was taken over by the Hudson's Bay Company which held absolute sway over the inland empire for the next thirty-five years. The fort was soon moved across the river to North Kamloops and later transferred to the south bank of the river, east of the present city.

The visitor travelling from the West Coast to the Interior often gets the impression that Vancouver and New Westminster were the province's first settlements, and that the frontier was pushed slowly inland. However, before the Lower Fraser River was even explored in the 1820s, Kamloops was the recognized center for a vast and profitable fur trade.

Catholic missionaries, known descriptively as "Black Robes," reached Kamloops in the 1830s. Perhaps the next significant development came in the early 1850s when an Indian appeared at the Fort with specimens of coarse gold. Their sale to the Chief Trader, together with rumors of other gold discoveries, resulted in the gold rush of 1858, and led to the founding of British Columbia.

Hearing of the immense riches in the B.C. goldfields, a group of prairie settlers banded together and started a perilous journey to this promising new country. The "Overlanders," as they were called, came by way of the almost unknown Yellowhead Pass and later, upon a difference of opinion as to routes southward, divided into two bands. The smaller party attempted to follow the North Thompson River where several perished in rapids, swamps, and dense forests. Their perilous trip's end, in October of 1862, was a matter of little excitement to personnel at the trading post who briefly recorded in their diary that "the Canadians arrived."

Among the "Canadians" who arrived was the only woman in the original party of 154. She was Catherine Schubert who was pregnant during the three-month ordeal of crossing the prairies and challenging the wilderness of the turbulent North Thompson River. A few hours after she, her husband and three children arrived at Fort Kamloops, Mrs. Schubert gave birth to a daughter, the first white child born in the Interior of B.C. (See Heritage House book, *The Overlanders of '62*.)

Some of these hardy people stayed as settlers and, through their pioneering efforts, contributed much to the stability of Kamloops as an early ranching center. One Overlander, William Fortune, pre-empted land and built the first flour mill in B.C., using two millstones that had been shipped around Cape Horn at a cost of $1,200. These millstones, now crumbling from age and exposure, are displayed at the Kamloops Museum.

Traffic from the Cariboo Road began to trickle in and, in 1870, Barnard's Express was running to Savona at the foot of Kamloops Lake. The service was soon extended to Kamloops but the big event was in 1885 when the CPR reached the community. In fact, for many years, the track ran down the main street of the town.

The townsite was properly surveyed and subdivided. Log buildings gave way to more modern and permanent structures and, in 1893, Kamloops was incorporated. Although other cities had been incorporated earlier, Kamloops is the oldest established city in British Columbia. Even at this early date, electric lights and a water system were in operation. The last major event took place in 1915 when the Canadian Northern Railway (now the Canadian National) was completed.

Backed by many years of steady and well-planned progress, Kamloops moves ahead in confident fashion. Despite the summer's heat and low rainfall, green boulevards and masses of bright flowers greet the visitor. Kamloops is headquarters for a large number of Provincial and Federal agencies. It has its own radio and TV stations, a beautiful riverside park, a museum, and all of the more general public services. The number and quality of its hotels and motels speak well for the favor this city holds with visitors.

LOCAL PLACES AND NOTES OF INTEREST:

**Visitors and Convention Bureau:** At 10 - 10th Avenue, the Bureau can supply information ranging from the location of the city's six shopping malls to

**Kamloops today and in the 1880s. The North Thompson, center, and the South Thompson, at right, meet to form the Thompson River.**

over forty motels, hotels and tent and trailer parks; from fishing lakes to points of interest. Open all year. Phone (604) 374-3377.

**Riverside Park** is located on the banks of the Thompson River one-half block from the downtown area. Includes some 2 miles (3.2 km) of pedestrian walkways, a sandy beach with clear unpolluted water, rose garden, huge shade trees, swimming pool, picnicking facilities with two kitchen shelters and lots of parking. Canadian National Railway's steam engine 2141 is an added attraction.

**Kamloops Museum,** 207 Seymour Street, features two floors of exhibits which make it one of the finest in Interior B.C. There are exhibits on all aspects of local history, including Indian culture, the fur trade, and the city's pioneer era. Includes a large collection of photos, manuscripts and maps. Open from Tuesday to Saturday, closed on Sundays, Mondays and statutory holidays. Phone 372-9931.

**Heritage Walk:** This loop walk through a few blocks of the downtown area can be completed in half an hour. It includes the Presbyterian Church, built in 1887 and the oldest public structure in Kamloops. Other buildings are the former City Hall, Provincial Courthouse, old homes and various official heritage sites. A good place to start is at the museum where a map with route description is available.

**Kamloops Exhibition Association:** The Association has been responsible for community events for over 100 years. The exhibition grounds have one of the best horse-race tracks in Western Canada with thoroughbred and quarter-horse racing and pari-mutuel betting all summer. Other events are the Provincial bull sale in March, the Provincial Winter Fair in late September and in mid-August the city's festival which features five days of exhibits and events.

**Weyerhaeuser Canada Tour:** An interesting two hours can be spent touring Weyerhaeuser's bleached kraft pulp mill. The huge complex each year turns some 700,000 tonnes of waste wood chips and sawdust into pulp for use in everything from writing paper to cellophane. For tour times, phone the mill at 372-2217 (Local 373).

**Fishing and Camping:** The Kamloops area is justifiably famous for the variety and number of lakes throughout the district, most of them containing resorts and many on a paved highway. Within a 75-mile (120-km) radius of Kamloops are some 200 lakes, so the choice can be bewildering, whether fishing fun is sought on a lake-a-day basis or whether a family vacation is to be spent at one of the resorts. Several sporting stores in Kamloops can provide current data on fishing conditions and an excellent brochure, *Fresh Water Sport Fishing*, lists some 50 resorts and the facilities each offers. This free brochure is available from the Visitors and Convention Bureau or by writing: B.C. Interior Fishing Camp Operator's Association, Box 3301, Kamloops, B.C., V2C 6B9.

The B.C. Fish and Wildlife Branch Regional Office is at 1259 Dalhousie Drive, Kamloops, V3C 5Z5. Phone (604) 374-9717.

**Paul Lake Provincial Park:** Set amid mixed fir and aspen, this major development is 6 miles (9.5 km) north of Kamloops on Highway 5, then 8 miles (12.8 km) eastward over a paved road. It contains 111 campsites, 58 picnic sites and a sani-station. Fair fishing for Kamloops (rainbow) trout which can top 6.5 lbs. (3 kg).

**Forest Service Recreation Program:** The B.C. Forest Service Recreation program is designed to provide access to lakes and establish recreation sites on them. These sites usually contain picnic tables, toilets, garbage containers and a boat launching area. In the Kamloops district, there are over 600 miles (1,000 km) of trails and over 300 recreation sites. For maps and more information contact Regional Office, Ministry of Forests, 1210 Summit Drive, Kamloops, B.C., V2C 1T8.

**City of Kamloops Lookout and Stop of Interest:** The Lookout, at the upper end of Columbia Street not far from the Trans-Canada Highway, is easy to access and provides a panoramic view of the city and the North and South Thompson Rivers. Directly northeast of the junction of the two rivers is Paul Peak and, almost straight behind, Peter Peak — 3,595 ft (1,080 m) — outdoing Paul in size and height. To the northwest are the barren Batchelor Hills and Lac du Bois where hundreds of horses were pastured during the fur-trade era over 150 years ago.

**Stop of Interest—** FUR, GOLD AND CATTLE: "Founded in 1812, Fort Kamloops stood at a natural crossroads. For 50 years it remained the focus of an inland fur empire until the roaring mining boom of the 1880s. Ranchers with cattle and horses replaced the miners. They settled, and stayed to see two railways bring prosperity anew to this land of sagebrush, sun and great rivers."

**Skiing:** In addition to the Lac Le Jeune area, there are two other developments near Kamloops — Harper Mountain and Tod Mountain.
Harper Mountain is 15 miles (24 km) from Kamloops via Highway 5. Facilities include a triple chairlift, two T-bars and a handle tow. Its eleven trails include two cross-country, one of them 5 miles (8 km) long.
Tod Mountain is 34 miles (54.4 km) from Kamloops via Highway 5. This complex has the longest double chairlift in North America, 2 miles (3.2 km). In all, facilities include one triple chairlift, two double, two platter and a rope tow. There are thirty-three runs, including 5 miles (8 km) of beginner family runs. Services include two day lodge cafeterias, two lounges and a ski shop. Summer visitors should check the Visitors Bureau for hours of service.

**Thus ends** the route description of the Fraser and Thompson River Canyons from Vancouver to Kamloops. Travellers bound for the Shuswap-Okanagan will find route information in Heritage House book, *Okanagan Valley*. For those heading eastward to Banff, Heritage House book, *Incredible Rogers Pass through Glacier National Park*, contains a description of the spectacular Selkirk Mountains between Revelstoke and Golden. Visitors heading northward over Highway 5 to Highway 16, then eastward to Jasper-Edmonton-Saskatoon-Winnipeg, or westward to Prince Rupert, will find route information in the three-volume Heritage House series, *Magnificent Yellowhead Highway*.

# A Selection of Other *Heritage House* Books

**HISTORIC FRASER AND THOMPSON RIVER CANYONS:** The Trans-Canada Highway from Vancouver to Kamloops is a unique route with scenery from mountains to sagebrush, wildlife from mountain goat to muskrat, vegetation from dogwood to cactus. Here is a 128-page guide — including its colorful history. **$7.95**

**B.C. PROVINCIAL POLICE STORIES:** For over 90 years from 1858 until 1950 the B.C. Provincial Police upheld the law. From official files here is a selection of the lawmen's most interesting adventures in mystery and murder. **$7.95**

**WILDLIFE OF WESTERN CANADA:** Over 100 illustrated panels on wildlife from the giant blue whale, at over 100 tons larger than the biggest dinosaur, to the pygmy shrew which weighs less than a soda cracker. **$8.95**

**THE PICK OF THE NEIGHBOURHOOD PUBS — A GUIDED TOUR IN BRITISH COLUMBIA:** There are over 230 of these home-like, folksy meeting places throughout B.C. In 160 pages with maps and photos here is a guide to some 100 of them. **$9.95**

**OUTLAWS AND LAWMEN OF WESTERN CANADA — Volume One:** Some of Western Canada's dramatic crimes. Includes Alberta Indian Swift Runner who ate his mother, brother, wife and six children; Saskatchewan's first stagecoach holdup; the 1880 death on duty of Manitoba's pioneer police chief; British Columbia's "Phantoms of the Rangeland," and many others. 128 pages, photos, maps. **$7.95**

**OUTLAWS AND LAWMEN OF WESTERN CANADA — Volume Two:** More of Western Canada's dramatic crimes. There is Jess Williams, in 1884 the first man hanged in Calgary; Saskatchewan's Almighty Voice whose murder of a policeman in 1895 caused six other deaths; B.C.'s Henry Wagner who in 1912 was hanged so quickly that he set a world record; and many others. 128 pages, photos, maps. **$7.95**

**TRAGEDIES OF THE CROWSNEST PASS:** In Canada no place equals the tragedies of the Crowsnest Pass on the Alberta-B.C. border. At Hillcrest a mine explosion killed 189 out of 235 men; at Frank a mountain collapsed, killing upward of 100 residents; and at Fernie a mine explosion killed 128 men. **$5.95**

**OKANAGAN VALLEY:** This guide reveals the many wonders of a valley of beaches and blossoms; wineries and history; sunshine and — perhaps — a genial Okanagan Lake resident called Ogopogo. 128 pages. **$7.95**

**TALES OF CONFLICT: Indian-White Battles and Massacres in Pioneer B.C.:** Contrary to popular belief, B.C. was not settled peacefully. Hundreds of whites and Indians died in murders and massacres from Vancouver Island to the Fraser Canyon, from the East Kootenay to the Chilcotin. 128 pages. **$7.95**

**STAGECOACH AND STERNWHEEL DAYS IN THE CARIBOO AND CENTRAL B.C.:** For 50 years from 1863 when the first stagecoach rumbled northward from Yale until 1921 when the sternwheeler *Quesnel* was destroyed in Fort George Canyon, colorful stagecoaches and sternwheelers served Central B.C. **$5.95**

**SLUMACH'S GOLD — In Search of a Legend:** Do the Coast Mountains some 40 miles northwest of Vancouver guard gold worth upwards of $100 million? **$3.95**

**INCREDIBLE ROGERS PASS:** In this 55-mile section of the Trans-Canada Highway over 200 men died keeping the CPR's main line open. Today snowsheds and artillery protect motorists from snowfall which can exceed 700 inches a year. **$3.95**

**THE HOPE SLIDE — Disaster in the Dark:** In the darkness 100 million tons of rock buried B.C.'s Southern Trans-Provincial Highway over 100 feet deep, engulfing motorists already trapped by a snow slide. **$3.95**

**THE OVERLANDERS OF 1862:** From Fort Garry the 150 gold seekers headed west in ox-carts for the goldfields of Cariboo, 1,500 wilderness miles away. Months later they arrived — speed 12 miles a day, five dead, the rest lucky to survive.  **$3.95**

**Bill Miner. . .STAGECOACH AND TRAIN ROBBER:** The famous Pinkerton Detective Agency called him " . . . the master criminal of the American West." In a lifetime of crime he stole some $250,000, including $7,000 during Canada's first train holdup in B.C. in 1904 — and escaped from every jail he was in.  **$4.95**

**THE RIEL REBELLION — 1885:** In 1870 Riel won the Metis representative government when the province of Manitoba was founded. In 1884-85 he again led the Metis. The results were tragic, with death to many — including Riel.  **$5.95**

**FROG LAKE MASSACRE:** On April 17, 1885, came a message from what is today Alberta: "There's been a massacre at Frog Lake. All the white men have been murdered and their wives taken prisoners by Big Bear's Plains Crees." This book describes the massacres, pursuit of Big Bear, and the experiences of nearly fifty prisoners living under daily threat of execution.  **$5.95**

**CHUCKWAGON RACING — Calgary Stampede's Half Mile of Hell:** Four wagons behind sixteen galloping horses chased by sixteen outriders makes chuckwagon racing one of the world's most dangerous sports. Born at the Calgary stampede in 1923, its heritage is the rangeland of the Canadian West.  **$4.95**

**The Death of ALBERT JOHNSON . . . Mad Trapper of Rat River:** One intriguing mystery remains in this saga of pursuit and shoot-out in the numbing cold of Canada's Arctic over half a century ago — WHO WAS ALBERT JOHNSON?  **$6.95**

**Gabriel Dumont . . . Jerry Potts — CANADIAN PLAINSMEN:** Had Dumont and Potts lived in the U.S., they would be as well known as Davy Crockett and Daniel Boone, frontiersmen whom Dumont and Potts equalled in skill and courage.  **$3.95**

**BANFF — PARK OF ALL SEASONS:** A 15-square-mile reserve around a Rocky Mountain hotspring in 1885 developed into Banff National Park. Today Banff covers over 3,500 square miles and hosts over three million visitors a year.  **$2.95**

**MAJESTIC JASPER:** Mt. Edith Cavell, Miette Hot Springs and Maligne Lake; wildlife from moose to mountain sheep; and year-round activities from skiing to hiking attract two million people yearly to this largest of Western National Parks.  **$2.95**

**WATERTON NATIONAL PARK:** The Indians knew it as "Land of the Shining Mountains," a unique area in southwestern Alberta where prairie meets the mountains and nature sculpted lakes and valleys against a snow-peaked background.  **$2.95**

**MAGNIFICENT YELLOWHEAD HIGHWAY — Volume One:** From Portage la Prairie to the Pacific Ocean, the Yellowhead is a panorama of prairie, plains and mountains. This volume describes 750 miles from Portage to Edmonton.  **$2.95**

**MAGNIFICENT YELLOWHEAD HIGHWAY — Volume Two:** From Edmonton 504 miles through Jasper National Park to the sagebrush country of B.C.  **$2.95**

**MAGNIFICENT YELLOWHEAD HIGHWAY — Volume Three:** From Mount Robson, the Rockies highest peak, westward 628 miles through some of North America's most scenic sport fishing country to tidewater at Prince Rupert.  **$2.95**

**STOPS OF INTEREST IN SOUTHERN ALBERTA:** Along Alberta's highways are over 100 historical markers that describe unique geographical features, events of historical significance and honor pioneers. Here are those in southern Alberta.  **$3.95**

**THE CYPRESS HILLS OF ALBERTA-SASKATCHEWAN:** Twenty miles wide, 200 miles long, nearly 5,000 feet high, they are a unique landform — ranking with the Grand Canyon and the desert of Western America.  **$3.95**

**GHOST TOWNS OF SOUTHERN ALBERTA — Volume One:** Silver City, Bankhead, Mitford, Brant, Cleverville and other communities were once home to thousands. Today they survive only in photos, newspapers and memories.  **$3.95**

**GHOST TOWNS OF MANITOBA:** During the surge of settlement scores of Manitoba towns were born. Scores also died. Some of them were Manitoba City, Bannerman, Odanah, Asessippi, Millwood, Ewart, Millford, Grand Valley, Dropmore and Hecla. Thirty-one chapters, over 100 photos, 160 pages.  **$9.95**

The above titles and others are available at bookstores and other outlets throughout B.C., Alberta, Saskatchewan and Manitoba. If not available order direct from Heritage House Publishing Company, Box 1228, Station A, Surrey, B.C. V3S 2B3. Payment can be by cheque or money order. Books are shipped postpaid.